WINNING THE "HEAD" GAME...

Key to Elite Athletic Status

Coach Sonny Smith
and
Lou Vickery

ISBN: 9798589830118

Upword Press, LLC
Fairhope, AL 36532

louvickery@louvickery.com

louvickerybooks.com

ADVANCE ACCLAIM FOR WINNING THE "HEAD" GAME

"While ***WINNING THE "HEAD" GAME*** is a sports book, it has application for real life learning. There is really little difference between sports and life--at the end of one is the beginning of the other."

-Chuck Ghigna a.k.a. Father Goose

"I was a head coach in high school football for forty-one years. My teams won 321 games. My 1988 team at Pine Forest High School, in Pensacola was the USA Today National Champion. I know something about motivation…and this book does the job in detailing motivation and inspiration. Every coach should have a copy on his desk."

-Carl Madison, Hall of Fame Football Coach, Florida and Alabama

"***WINNING THE "HEAD" GAME*** is designed to provide a spark when one is needed. The words found here will instruct… inform… inspire athletes to reach beyond their grasp and hopefully, snag onto something that will make their careers better."

-Floyd Adams, Hall of Fame Baseball Coach, Florida

"It has been 60 years since I pitched in the Major Leagues. I am surprised that most of the chapters in WINNING THE "HEAD" GAME are ageless. The advice still applies for any age...don't stop improving and growing post sports right on through career, family, and retirement. The book is inspirational and informative without lecturing. It says it exactly right! Well done. I highly recommend it.

Bill Wakefield, MLB Pitcher, California

"This just plain and simple is a great book both young athletes and those who coach them. It has more inspiring messages and lessons in it than any book of its kind I have ever picked up. I would highly recommend it to youth program coaches and athletics."

-Bev Mathis-Swift, Soccer Mom, Virginia

"Winning The Head Game" provides the foundational pillars required by athletes, coaches, and competitors of all kinds. Yes, it's a sportsbook, but for me, it is also a life and business handbook. As a former collegiate athlete, active tennis coach, tennis pro, and serial entrepreneur I found Lou and Sonny's book a treasure chest of knowledge, experience, inspiration, motivation, and sports and life wisdom. It has timeless truths that should be ingrained into every reader's heart and mind.

-Jeff Vaage, Coach and Entrepreneur, Iowa/Alabama

"WINNING THE 'HEAD' GAME is one of the most complete, thorough and detailed discussions of one of sports and life's greatest challenges! I call it The Mental Game on "The Sports Doctor" radio show. It was always a top subject that Lou and I would talk about in my monthly guest spots on his "Lou in the Morning" radio show! Coach Sonny and Lou have put together a real ge3m here--so valuable for athletes, sports parents and coaches at all ages and levels!"

Dr. Bob Weil, host of the nationally syndicated radio show, "The Sports Doctor," Illinois

WINNING THE "HEAD" GAME hits so many nails on the head it would be difficult to pick out just one nail to comment on. The reader can easily read segments when time avails itself and come away with a quick reminder. Great stuff that will be either new to the reader or a reminder of things they may have forgotten. A must read!!

-Aubrey Whitaker, Retired Coach, Florida

"As a human relations specialist, active amateur tennis player /teaching pro, and overall sports psychology "sponge," it takes a lot to grab and keep my attention. This book does it! I recently upgraded my professional tennis instructor certification status to "Elite." Little did I realize the endless possibilities that awaited me as Sonny and Lou really opened my eyes to what an "Elite" mindset could bring. Thank you, Lou and Sonny, for a great job!"

-Wendall Walker, Elite Tennis Instructor, Florida

THE LINEUP

FOREWORD

In Winning the "Head" Game, Coach Sonny Smith and Lou Vickery combine their talents and vast experiences in the world of sports and the entertainment industry to create this informative and inspirational book. They demonstrate ways that competitors from all walks of life—and with a myriad of aspirations—can develop a winning mindset, open the doors of opportunity, and achieve individual and team successes that could yield unimaginable results.

The authors remind us that every action begins with a thought and that the manner in which we respond to both seen and unforeseen circumstances separates winners from losers in sports and life. We are reminded by the authors that assessing our individual and collective talents, then developing them to their maximum potential, is paramount to enjoying a life defined by physical, psychological, emotional, and fiscal well-being.

To personalize the advice and admonitions they offer, each author shares personal examples of how he overcame adversity and by applying the life lessons shared in this book, turned aspirations into reality. To demonstrate that their own life experiences are timeless, cross-cultural barriers are reproducible, they also incorporate the winning ways of other successful coaches and athletes, from the world of sports. Their maxims on leadership, communication, and teamwork extend beyond athletic arenas and can be applied to any entrepreneurial endeavor… at every age.

E. Gaylon McCollough, MD FACS

EDITOR'S NOTE: Dr. Gaylon McCollough is a world-renown plastic surgeon and founder of the McCollough Institute for Appearance and Health. He was an academic All-American at the University of Alabama and played on the 1964 National Championship Football Team. Dr. McCollough was inducted in the Alabama Sports Hall of Fame in 2017 as a "Distinguished Alabama Sportsman." He is also an award-winning author of numerous books.

INTRODUCTION

We are excited that you have chosen to read WINNING THE "HEAD" GAME. Whatever it is that brought you to us, we are very thankful we can share this time with you. Hopefully, we can create a deep-felt desire on your part to explore in greater depth what it takes to become the elite athlete you may have only dreamed of becoming.

We sense by your being here, there is something unfinished--something you believe can be much bigger in your athletic journey. Our mission is geared toward providing the necessary ingredients to help you build a bridge from where you are to where you would like to go as an athlete. But you must truly believe in your heart that it will make a difference going forward.

We have drawn upon our many years of involvement in sports, at both the amateur and professional level, in structuring WINNING THE "HEAD" GAME. The motivational, inspirational, and informative messages in the book are a mixture of works that primarily apply to dealing with the "what" and "why," instead of the "how," of sports.

The book is structurally different. It is broken down into five parts. ***Part One: Sonny on Sonny*** is a brief autobiographical sketch by Sonny on himself. This affords you a chance to get up close and personal with him. It is a side of Sonny that very few people have been exposed to, or know about.

Part Two: Personal Readiness is directed toward the personal phase of how you view you. We would venture you see yourself as being capable of doing a lot of things very well, athletically speaking. Some other things you do are passable, and probably a few maybe not so good. It matters how you look at yourself, but more importantly, is how you view the unseen abilities and possibilities yet to come.

Part Three: Preparing for Action places the accent on the preparation of mentally and physically preparing what goes on between the white lines. We didn't write WINNING THE "HEAD" GAME for athletes based on their present athletic status and boundaries. WINNING THE "HEAD" GAME is written for those who see themselves as "a work in progress." Would that be a fair assumption about where you are in your athletic journey? Becoming an elite athlete is a developmental process. Our purpose is to help you move from potential to reality.

Part Four: Between the Lines offers some salient ideas for maximizing your efforts when the action begins for real. From creating activity to handling setbacks to overcoming defeat, this part of WINNING THE "HEAD" GAME focuses on what makes a difference when the game action is ongoing.

A real plus at the end of each chapter is what we call a **SONNY MOMENT.** the right mix of wisdom and relevant points of interest. There's plenty here for coaches and athletes. Coaches in particular will find some of the messages by Sonny to offer a very unique perspective.

Part Five: Overtime highlights the culmination of our mission to offer motivational and inspirational material that can keep you expanding and growing as an athlete. It is truly the end of a new beginning. You are ready to go.

Here's how we think you should use WINNING THE "HEAD" GAME. It is **a resource book.** For sure, you should read about Sonny's background in Part One. Then you can give the rest of the book the once over to discover where you will begin to focus your attention. However, it isn't the kind of book written with the intent of reading in one sitting. Instead, it is a book where you can read a particular chapter at any point in time that might apply to your personal circumstances.

A commitment to reading regularly is important. So, we encourage you to keep the book handy. See in your mind's eye the energy and power that can arise when you put the words to use. Our mission will be fulfilled if our words move you beyond what you have been for the greater reward of what you can become.

Good luck… and great success to you and your team!

Coach Sonny Smith and Lou Vickery

PART

I

Sonny on Sonny

Chapter One

SONNY: THE FORMATIVE YEARS

My story may very well someday be your story. I can attest that the breadth and depth of my career led me along a very unusual path. For sure, that path zigged and zagged, but the further I travelled, the straighter it got.

I have been immensely blessed. That's the one reason I wanted to take a little time at the beginning of the book to share some events of my personal life with you—even some things I have not publicly shared before. It is interesting to identify and recall some things that impacted the course my life has taken.

It was a different time and under different circumstances when I began my coaching journey from a little mountain town—Roan Mountain--in Tennessee. It was tough growing up there in the forties and early fifties. Although one of my first goals was to make the people of Roan Mountain proud of me, I really couldn't wait to move on.

Roan Mountain was a small town, with a population of about 1,000 people living there during my youth. You could easily double that number if you tossed in all the hunting dogs. I would venture the cartoon character, Snuffy Smith, was tailored after our Smith family. There are a lot of similarities from which to draw such a conclusion. Later on, after I went to college, my teammates starting calling me "Snuffy." It definitely fit.

Life in and around Roan Mountain was simple, but not necessarily easy. Most of the people were like us, incredibly poor. The best way to define my childhood would be that it was full of scarcity and austerity. We had little to nothing and did everything in our power to hold onto what we had. The theme in Roan Mountain was to make do with anything you could get your hands on. We raised our vegetables in a garden on the side of a mountain. Figure that one out!

Our home was a shack. You could look through the holes in the floor and see the dogs and through the broken windows at night and see the stars. I liked looking at the stars best. It gave me hope.

We had no electricity or running water in the house. Kerosine lamps and the fireplace were the sources for light. Irmie used the fireplace to cook. We had to travel about 60 yards down the mountain to a stream for water. It was a tough row to hoe, tracking back up the mountain trail hauling a bucket of water.

The fireplace supplied the heat in our house. I was six years old before I realized my name was not "Git Wood." I was at least fourteen before I learned that "hand-me-downs" was not a brand name.

This may surprise you, but I was called "Sonny" right from the get-go. The doctor who delivered me referred to me as "Sonny boy." The Sonny part stuck. Although I have a given name, I have answered to "Sonny" all my life. It amazes me that most folks today call me Sonny, not Coach.

Since we didn't have much money to spend on clothes and shoes, our mother made clothes for myself and my brother, Jim. Our mother was named Irma, but almost everyone called her Irmie. I can tell you that you couldn't find a better woman than Irmie. She was an unbelievably good lady and a pillar of strength for our family. She worked as a cook in the school system for years and made $14 per week when I graduated from high school. Yet, she saved up enough money to buy me a used car my last year in college. I was always proud of Irmie. I could not have asked a better mother.

I know the mentality and immense hurdles presented by a dysfunctional family. I lived them. I didn't always grasp everything ongoing between my father and mother, but my father, Grigg, would rarely treat Irmie right. I know she was continually frustrated by how he treated her and the little money he gave her to run a household. But she stuck with him.

Grigg was a different breed. Some would call him a disciplinarian. Others saw him as downright mean, including me. Grigg was known to pull his knife on anyone, including his family, to let all know who was in charge. Grigg was street smart and gifted with a persuasive tongue. He could have sold snow to an Eskimo.

Grigg held numerous jobs. At various times, he was a mill worker, moonshine whiskey runner, a deputy sheriff, and many other, primarily questionable jobs where he could make money. Think about the fact that he was breaking the law and sworn to keep the law at the same time. You see, Grigg came up with an imaginative way to keep the local law people at bay while running moonshine whiskey.

If you wanted to be sheriff in our county, you better get Grigg on your side. Grigg would help get a sheriff elected and then have the sheriff deputize him. As a deputy sheriff, he was always aware of plans to raid a moonshine operation he was involved with at the time.

While Grigg didn't have to concern himself with the local law enforcement, he still had to contend with the Federal revenuers. He had many close calls with them. The Feds searched our home on many occasions through those early years but never were able to catch Grigg with the goods.

The Federal boys would park their car down the mountain where they were hopeful we couldn't see them coming. But we were always on the lookout for them, and we could see them trekking up the path leading to our house. Irmie, Jim, myself, and Grigg (if he was home) would gather up all the jars of moonshine whiskey in the house and hide them in Irme's bed.

Irmie would then get in the bed and pretend to be sick--no checking there by the revenuers. It worked every time, although I think those old revenuer boys knew better. The man in charge would tell Irmie before leaving that he hopes she gets well before the next visit, but she never did when they came around!

It seemed like Grigg was always one step ahead of being caught. As far as I know, he was able to escape every time. He had to have a rabbit's foot in his pocket with all his strokes of luck.

Probably the number one skill of a good moonshine runner was driving a vehicle. To this day, I am a big NASCAR fan because my interest in racing began with moonshiners driving their souped-up vehicles by our place with the revenuers in hot pursuit. Some of the early NASCAR drivers got their start running moonshine.

I was about fourteen years old when Grigg purchased an old beat-up Plymouth that he would fix up to be his whiskey runner. There were rust spots all over the body, so Grigg got some paint and a couple of brushes for Jim and me to paint it. When we finished the paint job, Irme thought she saw a slight movement in the car. Since the car was parked on a slope, she asked me to check and see if it was in gear. I didn't know one gear from the other.

What happened next was equal parts scary and hysterical. I opened the driver's side door, slipped into the driver's seat, and proceeded to wiggle the gear shift that rose from the floorboard. Nothing. I got out of the car, thinking everything was okay. I had no longer made my exit when the car started to roll down the mountain. Through a fence and into a cornfield it went, picking up tassels and corn shucks on the still-wet paint. Fortunately, it came to a stop against the neighbor's wood cutting block, securing a few dents as it did.

What a sight to behold. We could laugh then, yet it would be anything but a laughing matter when Grigg got home. When he saw what had happened, Grigg began to bellow at the top of his lungs over and over. What he was saying was inaudible. Thank goodness. We scattered to Irme's parents' home. None of us wanted to wait around for the possible consequences. Grigg drove that old Plymouth with tassels and shucks flapping in the wind. It became quite a conversation piece.

Believe it or not, someone who didn't know how to drive tried to steal the old car. The thief never got more than a hundred yards down the mountain before plowing into another neighbor's yard. I can't remember, but I believe Grigg got a better car shortly after that. We did get a better home. Grigg built it himself. Period. Electricity, plumbing, the whole works. The man could make or fix anything. He also had an entrepreneurial eye.

For example, when the television first came out, Grigg came up with the idea of opening a TV repair shop. He learned just enough about televisions to be dangerous, but he devised the ingenious plan of taking parts from one customer's TV set, then he would insert those parts as needed in another customer's TV. Often, he had to wait on another TV to be brought in for repair since he didn't have an extra one in-house to use for parts.

How long that business lasted, I don't remember. But you get an idea of what kind of person Grigg was. Someone said at the time, "Grigg is a con man masquerading as an entrepreneur." He came by it naturally. My grandfather might have been worse. They both participated in the moonshine whiskey business and numerous other questionable enterprises where they could make a buck.

Not a soul had any clue how much money Grigg had. He didn't believe in keeping it in the bank so he would bury it here and there in the yard, and who knows where else. It wouldn't shock me if there is money still buried around the old homeplace.

Speaking of money, I had a difficult time keeping Grigg away from the money I earned from doing various jobs. He told me I owed it to him for "being kept up."

Grigg would not take a drink of liquor during the week, but he and a buddy of his named McNabb would get drunk every Saturday night. They would sit on the floor at our house, insisting Irme and I sing hymns for them while they drank moonshine whiskey. Irme would play the guitar, and we would sing until both Grigg and McNabb began to cry. We would go to bed and leave them both drunk on the floor.

There's a story about McNabb that says he got up one Sunday morning after drinking virtually all night and headed down to the church house, reeking of whiskey. On this occasion, his arrival at the church coincided with the services just ending, and the church attendees headed out to the creek behind the church for a baptismal service. McNabb was right in step with them.

After a couple of folks had been baptized, the preacher asks if anyone else wanted "to find Jesus." Out of the crowd and into the water steps McNabb. The preacher proceeds to dunk McNabb, and when he comes up, the preacher asked him, "Have you found Jesus?" McNabb answered, "No." After two more dunks and two more "Have you found Jesus?" questions, McNabb, who is almost out of breath now, struggled to ask the preacher, "Are ya shore tis is whair he fell in?"

Health Issues

I had numerous health issues as a youngster. It was not until my late teenage years that I developed greater resilience to a variety of ailments. The early teen years were my worst. I had rheumatic fever, a form of Rocky Mountain spotted fever, and various other health issues over my teen years. My health did not allow me to play sports with any element of consistency. I will tell you more about that a little later on.

I had two near-death experiences in my early teens. I remember well a Halloween night when I was thirteen years old. I had become extremely ill over the previous few days. Irmie kept telling Grigg that I needed medical attention. Finally, on Halloween night, Grigg told everyone to get in the car, he was going to drive me to the hospital. I was so sick that I had to be helped into the car.

*We had just started for the hospital when suddenly we encountered a Halloween prank. There were two outhouses stretched across the road. Without giving any appreciable thought to trying to find an alternate route, Grigg turned around and drove us home. It was a miracle that I survived. Without any medical assistance, my health continued to deteriorate. It didn't look good.

My condition got so bad off the family was called in because it didn't look like I was going to make it. I was a sick puppy. Irmie invited a Presbyterian minister by the name of Asa Gray, to come and pray for me. In a few days, I had turned the corner and my condition slowly began to show some improvement.

Asa Gray became a mentor for me. I was enamored by him. After I gained enough strength, I took a job as a janitor at his church so I could be around him. I found myself walking like he did, and I even tried to talk like him. I thought about someday going into the ministry.

Grigg ended my relationship with Asa. He had a falling out with a member of Asa's church and after Grigg had an altercation with that person, he forbid me to go back to the church. My relationship with Asa was over.

After that incident, I began to spend most of my spare time away from home with various relatives. My mother's parents were a joy to be around, so I spent a lot of time with them and my mother's sister, June. No question: I was afraid of Grigg. My younger brother Jim stood up to him, but I didn't. I tried to distance myself as much as I could from the oppressive ire of Grigg.

Let me say something about Jim. He was naturally funny. He could make you laugh at the drop of a hat. He was also a better athlete than me. He was an outstanding baseball player and a good basketball player. He could have gone to college and played, but he chose to remind in Roan Mountain. He never left.

During the period when I was spending a lot of time at home because of my health, I began a lifetime relationship with country music, notably bluegrass music. I became a big fan of Bill Monroe, Vern Gosdin, Sonny James, and the Osbourne Brothers, with whom I later became terrific friends. It was a rare Saturday that I didn't listen to the Grand Ole Opry on radio station WSM in Nashville. I would lay awake at night, dreaming of the day I would become a country music star and appear on stage to sing at the Grand Ole Opry.

Many years later, I got my opportunity to sing there. Jerry Clower, the noted comedian, and I had struck up a friendship. While performing on stage at the Opry one night, Jerry asked my radio partner and me at the time, Wimp Sanderson, to come up on stage. Wimp had coached at the University of Alabama when I was at Auburn. Rivals on the court and friends off may be the best way to describe our relationship. Our radio show, Sonny and Wimp, ran for six years in Birmingham. It did provide us both something to do and led to many speaking engagements all around our listening area.

Once Wimp and I were on stage, Jerry asked me to sing a song, any song. With all those University of Tennessee fans in the audience,

I chose "Rocky Top." The band leader asked me what key I wanted to sing in, but I didn't know anything about "what key." Be darned if he didn't select the highest key possible, and my rendition of "Rocky Top" was--to say the least--rocky. A few weeks later, I received a copy of the recording and a note from the producer. The message suggested that I may want to burn the recording. So much for my Opry career.

Aunt June encouraged my involvement with country music. She had aspirations herself of being on the Grand Ole Opry. She would play the guitar, and we would sing together many of the popular songs of that era and numerous ones she had written. We would perform in and around Roan Mountain, especially on the local radio station.

On occasion, Aunt June would take me with her to Bristol, Tennessee, to see some top Grand Ole Opry performers in concert. Bristol is said to be the birthplace of bluegrass music. I often wonder where Aunt June got the money to take me along. We would take a bus over to Elizabethtown, and then catch the train to Bristol. Those trips were quite a thrill for me...and I am sure, quite expensive.

High School Days

It was a miracle that I made it to Cloudland High School, given my medical history. I had grown straight up, like a beanstalk, tall and thin. My lack of bulk and stamina hindered my ability to be an effective participant in most sports while in high school. Baseball was the easiest sport for me to play. It wasn't easy playing basketball because of all the continuous running and movement. A lot of inaction in baseball allowed me the chance to catch a breather between plays.

I became a regular on the high school team, playing shortstop mostly. I was the best hitter on the team and was a speedy runner. An interesting sidebar about the baseball team, we did not have regular uniforms. We wore football pants without the pads in them furnished by the school. Each player had to furnish everything else. Most of the tops worn were T-shirts and football jerseys of various colors Some players wore shoes with cleats, if they could afford them. Some wore basketball shoes. Some wore no shoes. I think I did a little of all three.

I enjoyed playing baseball, mostly because I was pretty darn good at it. I often thought about one day playing in the major leagues. I followed many major league teams closely and could identify every position player on each major league team. During the summer, I played on an independent baseball team up in Marion, Virginia, where I led the batting average team. I played baseball for several summers and played well, but I never got an offer to play professionally. I do think I was good enough to play pro baseball, but the opportunity never arose.

I did go out for football--for one day. We only lived about 100 yards from the high school practice field. Grigg got word I was trying out for football. He came down to the practice field and made me take my uniform off right in front of the whole team and told me to go home in my skivvies. I couldn't believe what was happening. My brother, Jim, later retrieved my clothes from the locker room.

Grigg never said why he didn't want me to play football. As skinny as I was he might have thought I would get mangled, and it might cost him some money for medical reasons. All I know is that it was one of the most embarrassing moments of my life.

I did get to play some football while I was in college. Each year, an alumni team would play the high school team in an exhibition game. I played twice and scored six touchdowns on pass plays. I often wondered what would have happened if I had played football. I was tall and could run, a nice combination for a wide receiver. One of the players told me, I was so fast I could turn off the light switch and be in bed before the lights went out.

I had a great desire to play basketball that year. Clark Morton, my high school basketball coach had a tremendous influence on my life. Coach Morton pushed me to be somebody, not only on the basketball court but off the court as well.

I had high hopes entering my senior year of getting a scholarship, but again questions of health were an issue. In pre-season practices, I had an excellent eye for the basket. However, after a few times up and down the court, I would get fatigued. I didn’t have the physical stamina to last. I didn't have a first wind, must less a second.

I only played seven of the scheduled basketball games my senior year in high school. I had another stretch of bad health during the winter of that year, leading to an inability to play.

Obviously, I didn't receive any college basketball scholarship offers. I got well enough to play baseball in the spring. I played very well and thought I might have a chance to earn a baseball scholarship. Only a few colleges were offering them at the time, so I did not get a scholarship offer for baseball, either.

There was one thing outside of sports I truly enjoyed while in high school—acting. I was naturally funny and entertaining. I enjoyed making people laugh and enjoy being around me. I participated in every play, and after winning a talent show, I thought seriously about making a career as an actor.

I was also quite a prankster, to the tune that I was known around school as "Ole Crazy Sonny." This behavior might have been my way of glossing over what was happening at home. By the way, I never seriously pursued acting as a career.

Two very advantageous things happened as my high school graduation approached. My strength and confidence had grown dramatically to the point I was excited about playing either basketball or baseball in the summer. I finally decided to focus on basketball and set my sights on playing for a tema in an outstanding summer league. I felt I would have a better chance of earning a scholarship in basketball than in baseball.

Also, I did graduate. I didn't graduate magna cum laude, but I did graduate "Oh, Lordy." I was voted the most outstanding student by my classmates. Additionally, I was the first in my immediate Smith family to graduate from high school.

Without scholarship offers, the chance to continue my education at a four-year college was virtually nil. I guess I could have hit the eject button, but I didn't want to give up. My instincts told me to keep pushing forward, something good was going to happen. To this day, I believe great things transpire when you get into a pattern of believing great things will happen.

With my decision to play in the summer basketball league was still the hope of catching the eye of a college scout. I had gained some weight to go along with my improvement in strength and confidence. It was needed because these leagues were noted for their physicality. I played well, but neither a four-year nor a two-year college offered me a scholarship. It was disheartening. But my resolve was heightened. I told myself I would work even harder to prove the scouts were wrong.

The College Years

With no scholarship in hand, I enrolled in Lees-McRae College near my home in Roan Mountain. I went out for the basketball team, but failed to make the squad. Another setback, but it did little to deter from my desire to play college basketball.

My freshman year in college was quite uneventful. The highlight of that first year was my appendix ruptured while driving home from school. It turned out to be another touch-and-go health situation for me. I worked really hard at getting well enough before the summer basketball league began play, to be ready to play. When the season began, I was able to perform.

Surprisingly, that summer I was able to hold my own physically, and my shooting eye was dead on. In most games, I was either the leading scorer or the second-leading scorer on the team. After one excellent game, a stranger arrived at our home the following day and introduced himself as a representative of Holmes Junior College in Mississippi. He offered me a basketball scholarship on the spot. Irmie signed it for me.

I had only a few weeks to get my affairs in order, before heading to Mississippi and a brand-new beginning. Although I hated to leave Irmie and my brother Jim, I certainly wasn't going to miss Grigg.

I was excited about the prospects of what lay ahead. It was a step I was prepared and ready to take. There is always a part of us I think that enjoys the challenges of something different and exciting. I was headed to a striking, even remarkable new chance to exploit my talents.

Everything I owned in the world I packed into a paper bag for the trip to Mississippi. I was soon on my way to Goodman, Mississippi, and a fresh start. I only went home once, which was during Christmas break, I thumbed a ride to Roan Mountain and then back to Goodman.

I did well at Holmes Junior College, athletically. I can't say the same for academics. My goal was to make good enough grades to stay eligible. I was the leading scorer on the team the one year I was there. We won the championship for the Mississippi Junior College League, and I made the all-state team. I was later inducted into the Holmes Hall of Fame and the Mississippi Junior College Hall of Fame. Quite an honor, and entirely unexpected for only playing one year.

I also played baseball at Holmes. An unusual thing occurred during one of the games. I chewed Beech-Nut tobacco while playing, which was quite common for ballplayers in those days. During a particular game, from my position at shortstop, the only chance I had to catch a pop fly behind me was to make a lunge for it. As I fell to the ground, I swallowed the whole wad of chewing tobacco. It almost choked me to death. And talk about sick. I was beyond sick. That ended my tobacco chewing days.

You would have thought by the way I played at Holmes, I would have received a bundle of basketball scholarship offers from four-year colleges. I talked to Babe McCarthy, the famed coach at Mississippi State, and he did not hesitate in telling me I was too physically weak to play major college basketball. At six feet, three inches, weighing 150 pounds soaking wet, this appeared to be the sentiment for other major basketball programs. I ended up with just one offer from Southeastern Louisiana College. That offer didn't excite me, so I went home with a lot of trophies but no scholarship.

It's not enough to simply have a dream, but you have to pursue it actively. The second summer after graduating from Holmes, I returned to play in the AAU summer league. Again, a twist of fate brought life to my vision of playing college basketball. It grew out of another stroke of good fortune. Two local folks in Roan Mountain, Warren and Milburn Heaton, encouraged an oil distributor from Johnson City by the name of Steve Lacy, to pay my way to Milligan College, so I could play basketball. Mr. Lacy, whom I did not know, paid my two years tuition to attend Milligan. I saw Mr. Lacy's generosity as a loan and tried to pay it back over the years. Most checks written to him went uncashed. To this day, I do not know the reason behind his generosity.

Milligan College, a private Christian liberal arts college, is located near Elizabethton in Carter County, the same county where Roan Mountain is located. I haven't mentioned it, but Roan Mountain is 6,295 feet above sea level, the second-highest peak next to Mount Mitchell in North Carolina, east of the Mississippi River. The town of Roan Mountain was a couple of thousand feet above sea level.

Most summers, I did grunt work. I would clean yards, mow grass, pick up trash, and anything else I could make a buck doing. Between my junior and senior years at Milligan, I did something different. I set up a business at Rhodendron Garden, a tourist attraction which was located about 6,000 feet high up Roan Mountain. I paid $50 for a license, and to my surprise, Grigg built me a hut to provide cover for selling my hot dogs, hamburgers, drinks, and various souvenirs.

I did okay in my first venture into the business world. My hamburgers were pretty darn good, and the souvenirs I sold were the leftovers that I bought for pennies on the dollar from the 5 and 10 cent stores here and there. It was a great experience for me.

I did very well athletically at Milligan, not so well academically my first year. A teammate of mine at Milligan was Del Harris, who coached in the National Basketball Association. Del and I were best buddies. We served each other as "best men" at our respective weddings. He asked me many times to join him in the professional ranks as an assistant coach. It was a tough decision to make, but I preferred the college game. Later on, I will share another story featuring Del.

The nickname for Milligan was "Buffaloes." I doubt if there were ever any buffaloes in the area. The college campus was located near Buffalo Creek in Carter County, and the original school's name was the Buffalo Male and Female School. I often wondered about the name of the creek, but never asked anyone about it.

We had a great basketball team my senior year. Del and I led the team in scoring every game. I began to seriously believe I was playing well enough to have a chance to play pro basketball.

My academics also really changed after I started to date Jan, my wife of sixty years. We met at the end of my first year at Milligan. So, the more I was around Jan, the greater my interest soared. She was an easy person to talk to, and she was steadfast about me and my grades. I was surprised by how much Jan had learned about sports. Later on, in my coaching career, she understood basketball so well, she occasionally offered me some daggone good coaching advice. Jan became a great student of the game over the years.

I made the Dean's List my last semester. You read that right. I had to do it to graduate. Jan was very instrumental in that being a reality. She stayed on my fanny and pushed me beyond a level I had never been academically. It felt good, and I graduated. Jan and I got married three months after I received my degree in education.

"Okay. Now, what's next? That was on my mind now.

Chapter Two

SONNY: THE COACHING YEARS

Sitting around dreaming about what we hope to be offers little movement toward becoming what we want to be. One of the easiest things to do is to find excuses why we cannot do something. Elsewhere in the book, you will find this quote: "Let your actions speak louder than your excuses." We can tell ourselves we are too unskilled, too untalented, too unworthy, too young, too old, too unknown, too unconnected, to set in our ways to make the necessary steps in establishing a path to where we want to go and what we want to do when we get there. Our excuses sit right at the core of what holds us back from reaching out to maximize potential.

Through my early years, I had fantasized about being a professional baseball or basketball player, a minister, a county music singer, and an actor. While I think I had talent in these areas, I wondered if I would be overmatched and end up being humiliated by any of those choices. There was a battle between logic and emotion that waged on the inside. But as I got older and more mature, I could sense a momentum shift toward something that would make my life feel more meaningful. That was coaching.

Before I would embark on a coaching career, my heart was still set on playing professional basketball. I was, in a way, trapped by the desire to play a few years before focusing on a coaching career. Coaching could wait. Playing could not.

I anxiously continued to chase the dream of being a professional player in the newly organized American Basketball Association. The summer after graduating from Milligan, I played on an Industrial League basketball team that was a part of a pro exhibition tour with Rod

Thorn and numerous other top professional prospects. I led the team in scoring. Although I outscored several players who did get the chance to play in the ABA, I wasn't offered a contract.

As much as I tried to rebuff the feelings of rejection, they were real. I tried to shake these feelings by telling myself I could prove them all wrong. All I needed was a chance. How could I convince the pro team scouts I had what it took to succeed as a player? The only thing standing between me and being a successful professional player was an opportunity. How could I possibly find a way to come face-to-face with that opportunity?

You know, there is nothing more American than opportunity. Opportunity comes in many forms and in many ways. On a rare occasion, an opportunity simply falls into our laps. But more often than not, we have to create our opportunities. As hard as I tried to create the opportunity to be a player, it didn't look like it would be a reality. It hurt. A deep-felt dream was going unfilled.

My gut feeling told me it was time to move on, but I was still stifled by my unwillingness to let go of the inner drive to play, not coach. To keep the lights on and put Jan's great cooking on the table, it was time to shift my thoughts into coaching full-time and assume ownership of my coaching destiny.

High School Coaching

I took my first coaching job at Lowgap, North Carolina. Lowgap sounds small, doesn't it? Believe me, it was smaller than that. I was the head basketball coach for both boys and girls. We had only one ball. It was not leather, but rubber. We shared it between the two teams.

I also coached the baseball team at Lowgap. Mixed in among my coaching duties, I was still actively playing basketball, searching for an opportunity to play professionally somewhere--anywhere.

The following year, I moved from Lowgap to Sparta, North Carolina to be the boys' head basketball coach. But the desire to play professionally was still prevalent in my thoughts. I only stayed one year at Sparta. I took an assistant coaching job at Marion, Virginia, the following year. There I could both coach and play for money on the Pepsi Cola team. I was paid $25 a game at some tournaments. I led the Pepsi team in scoring, but again, no contact. Not even a nibble.

I asked myself, “Is it finally time to get serious about coaching?” Jan felt it was. The decision was made, I was ready to throw myself entirely into coaching. I felt I had a gift for coaching, and now was the time to pursue that gift.

I think I was born to coach. I didn't want to be stuck behind a steering wheel each morning, commuting to a job that I knew would leave me emotionally disconnected. I knew many who had taken positions where they always appeared to be unhappy. I saw others who had lost their way or felt there was no other way to go except fall into the 9-to-5 routine. I just couldn't see myself chasing a career where the odds would be stacked against me. My heart wouldn't be in it.

During the early years, I would be hard-pressed in coaching and teaching to fulfill the obligations I had to my family. It was a struggle as we lived from pay check to pay check. Generally, by the end of the month, we would be flat broke. I found myself mentally hustling to find a way to move up the coaching ladder into a better-paying position.

After two moves in two years, I was ready to launch a more dedicated journey down the coaching path; I had a calling I wanted to fulfill and a family to support. My direction was established. Any thoughts of playing professionally were now in the background. I was off to be the best coach that I possibly could become.

The hotbeds for high school basketball in those days (and still today) were Indiana and Kentucky. Jan and I decided that getting serious about coaching meant finding a job to improve my resume. So, I accepted an assistant coaching position where basketball was king–Crawfordville, Indiana-- and worked under Dick Baumgardner, one of the best high school coaches in the game. That year was a great experience for me as I learned **how** to coach.

The following school year, my old high school coach, Clark Morton, who had become principal at Pine Knot, Kentucky High School, offered me a job as head basketball coach. I accepted. Kentucky was also a big-time basketball state that could enhance my resume. I only stayed at Pine Knot for one year. Then it was back to Marion, Virginia as head coach at Dublin County High School. I was there for two years. After the first year, I had agreed to be the head coach at Hot Springs, Virginia, but changed my mind. Hot Springs won the state championship that year.

While at Marion, our son, Steve, was born. Steve grew up to be an excellent athlete, playing several sports in high school. He was also an outstanding student, obviously taking after his mother in that regard. Steve played basketball at Milligan liked I did.

To this day Steve and his wife, Kathy, live in Johnson City, Tennessee, and have blessed Jan and me with two beautiful granddaughters, Stacy and Ryan, We also have three gorgeous great-granddaughters. Stacy is mother to two of three great-granddaughters, Lulu and Sonnie. Ryan birthed the other great-granddaughter, Emmie.

Next we were off to Bassett, Virginia, home of the furniture people. I was there for two years. I signed a contract to be the head coach at Radford, Virginia. I spent all summer getting the team ready to go, then came my opportunity to get into college coaching. That was in the summer of 1969. Radford team went on to win the state championship.

I fractured my forearm while playing basketball during the last winter at Bassett. I got a couple of small boards to create a homemade cast, put tape around the boards to secure them, and then placed a football pad over my arm. I did this during the game and continued to play. After the game, Jan had to drive me up a mountain to a hospital for medical attention. That incident was probably the last nail in the coffin for my playing days.

Our daughter, Sheri, was born while we were in Radford. Sheri today is a speech pathologist. She acquired a lot of experience assisting Jan after her massive stroke (details later), teaching her mother how to talk again. Sheri and her husband, Michael Wood, have two daughters, Mallory and Taylor. Neither of these granddaughters have children. It's nice for Jan and I that Michael and Sheri live in Auburn. That makes it convenient for us since that's where we now live.

Back to my college coaching quest. I worked at the Duke University basketball camp during the summers under the legendary Vic Bubas, the Duke University head basketball coach. I met Coach Bubas when I spoke at the Virginia State High School clinic. He also was there to speak. He told me after the clinic that I should be a college coach. I told him that I wanted to be. He added that if I would come and work at his camp, he would help me get a college job. That created a lot of inner excitement for me.

At the end of the second summer, I reminded Coach Bubas of what he had said about assisting in getting me a college job, and I asked him why he had not mentioned it again. "Because you haven't asked," was his answer. The pursuit of a college job was no longer a dream. It was on its way to becoming a reality.

I learned a valuable lesson with Coach Bubas. If you want something, ask for it. My cohort in writing this book, Lou Vickery, has written that ASK is an acronym. The A stands for Attitude. The S stands for Skills. The K stands for knowledge. Armed with a great attitude, superb skill set, and ample knowledge, why shouldn't we ask for something we want? With the ASK tools, we are ready to undertake a new challenge when it presents itself.

By the way, Coach Vic, and Bones McKinney, who was the immortal coach at Wake Forest at that time, both made a real impact on my coaching style. They were not only super coaches but outstanding people as well.

Coach Vic gave me the phone number of Warren Mitchell at William and Mary College. I immediately called him, and he offered me the job over the phone. Coach Bubas' recommendation had done the job. I replaced the famous Hubie Brown as an assistant coach at William and Mary College.

I moved around so much that Bill Cates, sports editor of the Roanoke Times, wrote an article about me. In the article, Bill referred to me as, "Suitcase Sonny." You would have thought I was trying to stay one step ahead of my creditors, which is probably the truth. After six stops in ten years at the high school level, I was ready for college.

College Coaching

Finding a little more stability didn't occur during the first two years in college coaching, either. After one year as an assistant at William and Mary, Gary Colson, coach at Pepperdine in California, offered me an assistant's job that doubled my pay. After only one year on the west coast, we loaded up and moved back to Virginia, where I took an assistant's job with Virginia Tech (VT).

I spent five years at VT as an assistant to Don Devoe before getting a shot at my first head coaching job. By then, I had gained a reputation as a good recruiter and teacher of fundamentals. While at VT, we won the National Invitational Tournament (NIT), which was a big deal back then. We won 4 games in 4 days.

After our second win, I flew from New York to Abilene, Texas to interview for a head coaching job at West Texas State University. I was offered the job, which I turned down. Then I flew back to New York for the NIT game the next day.

After winning the NIT, Don Devoe did not return to Virginia with the team, opting to fly to the NCAA basketball championships. The team and the rest of the coaching staff flew back to Roanoke, Virginia, where several thousand people greeted us at the airport.

In the absence of Coach Devoe, I climbed on top of a police car to address the crowd. After speaking for a few minutes, I asked each of the players to climb atop the car, one at a time. After the last player had been introduced, the players begin to chant for the team trainer to climb up to be introduced. He was big enough to qualify as a Sumo wrestler and had to be assisted by numerous players onto the car. Once he was on top of the car, the roof of the car caved in! It was funny, but not funny if you know what I mean.

Frank Mosley, the athletic director at VT, called me into his office a few days later. He wanted to know how I planned to pay for the damage to the police car and the team dinner that I had charged to the university after our arrival back to Roanoke. I told him where to go, and I would provide him a road map to get there. A fan paid for the repairs.

I had been a go-between for some time between Mosley and Devoe. To say they didn't like each other is an understatement. I was the popular choice to replace Devoe if he left VT. It would be difficult for Mosley to fire Devoe, given the success he had at VT. But when I announced my departure from VT for my first head coaching job, Mosley did just that. He fired Devoe.

Let me step back a bit to tell you about a pro coaching job offer I received while I was an assistant at VT. I was offered the head coaching position for the Grenoble, France pro team in Europe. I accepted the position, but four days before we were to depart for France, I backed out of the commitment.

The owner of the Grenoble team called me and told me I had the responsibility of finding a coach for the team. My college buddy, Del Harris, had been searching for a better coaching job, so I called to see if he would be interested. He was. Del accepted the job and was on his way to Grenoble.

Now, for the rest of the story. Numbered among the coaching staffs in the European League was the staff of the Utah Stars in what was then the American Basketball Association. After the European season ended, Del was offered a coaching position on the Stars staff. He accepted and went on to enjoy a stellar career in the pros including being the head coach for three National Basketball Association teams—Milwaukee Bucks, Los Angeles Lakers and Houston Rockets.

As I mentioned earlier in the chapter, Del approached me many times about joining him in the NBA. I was tempted, but the college game was more to my liking.

My first college head coaching position was at East Tennessee State in Johnson City, Tennessee, near my old hometown of Roan Mountain. The great Jerry West went with me to the interview for the ETSU job. Jerry and I had become friends when I worked at his basketball camp in the early part of the 1960s. He encouraged me to take the ESTU job, and I did. For years Jerry and I communicated regularly. He often tried to get me to take a coaching job in the pros, but it was never a good fit for me.

Two of my fellow assistant coaches at VT went with me to ETSU, Lawrence Johnson and Mack McCarthy. Jim Hallihan was my third assistant coach. While at ETSU we were 30-23 over two seasons. We won the Ohio Valley Conference Championship my second year. Johnson City was a place that my family grew to love.

Then I got the call from Auburn after Paul Lambert's untimely death. Paul had recently taken the job at Auburn and was temporarily staying in a motel in Columbus, Georgia. The motel was in the process of redo which included installing new mattresses. The old mattresses were stacked against the hallway walls. A fire started in one of the old mattresses and spread immediately to others. Paul perished from smoke inhalation. That was in June of 1978.

Taking the Auburn job was not an easy decision from a family standpoint. Jan and the kids did not want to leave Johnson City. Saying "yes" to Auburn meant our son, Steve, who would be a senior in high school that year, would remain in Johnson City to be a part of the sports teams and so he could graduate with his friends.

I took the Auburn head coaching position with the understanding that I would retain the assistant coaches that Paul had hired. One of those assistants, Herbie Greene, who had played at Auburn, stayed with me for 11 years. Herbie went on to a stellar coaching career as the head coach at Columbus State University in Columbus, Georgia. The floor of the arena at Columbus State was named for Herbie. He died at a much too young age.

Lawrence Johnson and Mack McCarthy joined me as assistant coaches at Auburn. Lawrence remained an assistant for me the rest of my coaching days, and today remains one of my dearest friends. Mack left Auburn to become the head coach at the University of Tennessee at Chattanooga. Mack also has been a close friend all these years.

I was at Auburn for 11 years. Someone wrote that my hire changed the course of the Auburn basketball program. By the 1983-84 season, we were in the hay days of the Charles Barkley era. That was the year that Auburn made its first-ever NCAA tournament appearance.

From that beginning, we had a lot of "firsts." We had three straight

20 win seasons, participated in the NCAA tournament for five consecutive seasons, from 1984 to 1988, and won a Southeastern Conference Tournament Championship. We also had three NBA lottery picks for successive years.

Many older Auburn fans have described the stretch from 1985-1988 as the most successful for the three major sports: football with Pat Dye, baseball with Hal Baird, and basketball with myself, in Auburn sports history. In examining the records, that is a high probability. It was a great time to be an Auburn Tiger fan.

Outstanding achievement at Auburn was the ability to develop talent for the next level of play. Having three first-round NBA draft choices—Charles Barkley, Chris Morris, and Chuck Person—was a real deal. Barkley became a star and was the NBA's MVP in 1993, Morris and Person became stalwart NBA players. That trend continued when I went to VCU, with several players becoming NBA players.

I resigned as coach after a dismal 1989 season, one which was marred by off-the-court issues and the threat of a possible investigation by the NCAA. Nothing materialized with the NCAA and I was cleared of any wrongdoing. I had serious regrets about the decision to leave Auburn for it was great for my family. But at the time it appeared the thing to do. I left for the head coaching job at Virginia Commonwealth University in Richmond, Virginia.

The Day Tragedy Struck

There are times in athletics–as well as life--that we never forget. There are special times and unexpected events that we can recall exactly where we were and what we did. There was a tragic event in the life of the Smith family that truly rocked our world. My wife Jan had a massive stroke at the age of 47 while we were at Auburn.

The day started no different than most. But it changed dramatically when I received the phone call announcing Jan's stroke. It shook my world. My first belief was this cannot be true. Maybe I had heard wrong. Maybe the doctor had made an erroneous diagnosis. Could it have been something else? Here was Jan in the prime of life, struggling to live and quite frankly, I felt hapless. There was nothing I could do.

The stroke caused Jan to lose access to her memory. Her motor skills were dramatically affected. She couldn't verbally communicate. It was the most devastating thing that had happened to me. It did not look good for her or our family.

While these were trying moments, they were always followed by moments of hope and positive expectations. The inward motivation to do whatever it took to get her well was deeply entrenched. It is amazing the recovery she made over the years. She overcame many stumbling blocks and worked her way back to virtually total health. Sheri was highly instrumental in Jan's recovery.

One of Jan's ideas to improve the use of her brain was to daily put together a crossword puzzle. She has worked at putting puzzles together all these years. You cannot imagine how painful it has been over the years to watch this amazing woman slowly and methodically arrange these puzzles into a semblance of order.

Jan was a vital part of our basketball program at Auburn. Charles Barkley, in a joint interview he and I did with Jeff Goodman on his podcast, may have said it best. "Sonny has the greatest wife ever," Barkley said. "…Mrs. Smith treated us all like sons. It was so awesome to have a mother figure close to you."

Countless players over the years felt that way about Jan. It is worth noting that Charles spent considerable time with Jan during her extensive hospital stay, as did many other players.

One of Jan's stroke repercussions occurred in the fact she could no longer handle all financial matters. Up to that point, I cannot recall ever having to write a bank check. Our daughter Sheri and I took on taking care of the finances, notably the bills.

To demonstrate my lack of proficiency in paying bills, I spent the full amount on the credit card bills, not aware that I didn't have to do that. For a good laugh, I was paying the total amount on a credit card bill without knowing how much money was in the bank. I had so many overdrafts that I had to make a loan at the bank to cover them. It is a laughing matter now, but it wasn't at the time.

On to VCU

My friend, Jimmy Taylor went with me for the interview at VCU. He told me to sit in the waiting room while he went behind closed doors to negotiate on my behalf. He emerged with a contract in hand that gave me a big raise over my Auburn salary, plus a new Cadillac car for both Jan and me. I couldn't believe it. I can assure you Jimmy did a much better job negotiating than I would have.

I spent nine years at VCU as head basketball coach and a year as an Assistant Athletic Director. My 1996 VCU team won the conference and tournament titles and the Rams went to the NCAA Tournament for the first time in eleven years.

I retired from coaching following the 1997-98 season. The AD at VCU asked me to pick my successor. I chose Mack McCarthy to replace me. Mack had been a long-time assistant of mine in the past.

I finished my college coaching career with 339 career victories in 22 seasons as a Division I head coach. I was coach of the year in every league that I had coached in, twice in the Southeastern Conference (SEC). I have been told that I am the only coach who won Coach-of-the-Year awards in five different conferences. Two other notable things were the colleges where I coached were never put on probation, and I was never fired from a coaching job.

I spent forty-plus years coaching and was blessed with so many wonderful coaching memories and making so many great connections. I still get goosebumps today thinking about them.

Final Word on Coaching

Basketball became a game of egos and individualism in my latter years of coaching. I did my best to stay true to being humble and shaking hands with folks as if I had known them forever. It was always very important for me to make everyone I met feel good about themselves. It has also been a significant part of my makeup to cheer folks up when I could see the sadness in their eyes. A poll conducted of college coaches by the Denver Post stated, "His peers selected Sonny Smith as the funniest man in sports." I think that part of me was a blessing for a lot of people. I still try to be that way today.

I saw basketball as only a game. It was not a matter of life or death. Whether my team won or lost didn't mean much in the larger scheme of things. If any coach realizes that going in, it is easier to face up to the adversity that a coach at any level is bound to encounter …and, in the end, a coach will be better off for it.

The most gratifying part of coaching is watching the young men under your tutorage develop and grow as human beings. I am still blessed with countless former players who stay in touch. Heart-warming, to say the least. It also is a wonderful feeling to see the number of former players who have done so well.

Chapter Three

SONNY: AFTER COACHING

It was not easy walking away from coaching. I had a bit of transition serving in an administrative position at VCU for a year after retiring as the basketball coach. But I was able to leave coaching on my terms. One reporter said this about my retirement: "Sonny Smith leaves the game as he entered it. A fun-loving, down-home friend to all he meets, incredible sense of humor, caring personality, and with the ability to coach the game of basketball, will be sorely missed."

Jan and I decided we would settle in Birmingham after leaving Richmond. NASCAR racing, country music, the Grand Ole Opry, and a lot of tennis were destined to occupy my time. I was able to expand my involvement with NASCAR as a speaker at many events. By the way, I had worked as a member of Dale Earnhardt's pit crew at the Winston 500 in 1985.

Before Jan and I were fully settled in Birmingham, opportunities to do a radio show five days a week and become a color analyst for TV basketball games became realities. With so much on my plate, instead of being retired, I thought I had become retarded.

Radio and TV

I had the reputation of having to be dragged out of the interview rooms when I was coaching because we had a plane or bus to catch. I had a great relationship with the media. The press people had a job to do, and I was willing to accommodate everybody in the press room. Win or lose, if I hadn't answered enough questions, I would invite the writers over to my home after home games.

I believe this interviewing experience paid big dividends when my old buddy, Wimp Sanderson, and I decided to host a sports talk show. The show ran for six years and was extremely popular. We had great guests, given both of us knew a ton of people from the sports world. The show was cancelled in 2006. We simply were making too much money, according to the powers above us.

Doing the show with Wimp was a lot of fun, and we attracted a big listening audience. But the cancellation of the show was no great disappointment. I had grown tired of making the drive-in bumper-to-bumper traffic each weekday. At the time, I was working as a basketball TV color commentator for Atlantic Sun games on the College South Sports Network. I did this from 2003 to 2014.

Sheri and her family had moved to Auburn, so in 2011 Jan and I moved there. For a while, I kept working as a commentator on the televised basketball games, traveling all over the south. Then the opportunity arose to join Rob Bramlett on the radio broadcast of Auburn basketball on the Auburn Sports Network. I didn't have any idea that I would be doing Auburn basketball when we moved to Auburn. I didn't go after them; they came after me. I accepted.

Rob and I had great chemistry. We had personalities that blended well together. I enjoyed a highly professional and personal relationship with Rob until he and his wife, Paula, died tragically in an automobile accident in May 2019. His loss hit me like a ton of bricks. So tragic.

The years I have been a commentator at Auburn have been enjoyable. I am working with Andy Burcham on the broadcast now. Andy is an easy guy to work with. I think he and I are on the same page during a broadcast. I believe he respects me for my ability to dissect a game as it unfolds. One of the things that makes broadcasting so much fun is I have a front-row seat.

I am known for my excellent preparation for a game. Well, that is probably a real stretch of the truth. Besides taking a look at the stats for each team before a broadcast, I pretty much wing it. It appears to work, although it makes some broadcasters I work with, a tad nervous.

I am often quizzed about Bruce Pearl, the Auburn head basketball coach. Bruce is the best practice coach I have been around. He is very good at teaching defense and the three-point shot. Bruce gives his players a lot of freedom on the floor, but the one thing that stands out to me about him is his ability to instill confidence in his players. He is always encouraging them, and I believe his players have respect for the way he believes in them and permits them to ad-lib a bit during a game

Speaking

I learned early on that I had a natural talent for telling a good humorous story. When I was at Virginia Tech, I begin to have more and more speaking opportunities. Don Devoe, the head coach, would rarely speak to any kind of group. He would ask me to step in for him, so I spoke at many basketball camps and banquets.

One opportunity, in particular, boosted my speaking career. Our Virginia Tech team was playing in Oklahoma City in the All-College Tournament. Coach Devoe asked me to speak in his place for a pre-tournament event. I did. I got on a roll telling stories, and it was a hit for all. Abe Lemons, the coach of the host school, Oklahoma City University, was noted at the time as the funniest man in basketball. The next day, the local newspaper headlines referred to me as "THE SECOND COMING OF ABE LEMONS." This opened up many speaking opportunities.

The deeper I got into my coaching career, the more I found myself doing speaking engagements. As I became more widely known in the speaking business, I branched out, speaking to larger and larger groups. While most were at coaching clinics all over the country, there were ample opportunities to do motivational talks in the business world. I spoke to employees of many major corporations. Even today I get inquires from groups wanting me to speak at their business conferences or corporate meetings.

When Wimp Sanderson and I were doing our radio show, we would speak in tandem to sports-related groups, mainly around the state of Alabama. I think we had a sign that read, "WILL SPEAK FOR FOOD." No. I am just kidding. I enjoyed those occasions. We ate good, and folks got their fill of a lot of stories and great laughs. Truth be known, I miss those occasions.

Honors

It is truly humbling the number of honors I have received over the years. I have been selected to eight Hall-of-Fames. Being selected to the Alabama Sports Hall-of-Fame was a real surprise. A bigger surprise occurred recently when I was selected to my home state of Tennessee's Sports Hall-of-Fame. Years ago, I had been a bit shocked when the gymnasium at my old high school of Cloudland in Roan Mountain was named for me.

As I mentioned earlier, it was an unbelievable honor to be named at least one time as the Coach-of-the-Year in every basketball conference that I coached in, and twice in the Southeastern Conference at Auburn. Ironically, I won three Coach-of-the-Year awards at VCU in three separate conferences—Sun Belt, Metro, and Colonial Athletic--while I was there.

Meeting Lou

My counterpart in the writing of this book, Lou Vickery, is a former professional baseball player, turn writer. Lou is a true wordsmith. He writes from his heart. You will see what I mean.

Our relationship started on the tennis court. We both loved being competitive, and we have won a lot of matches together over the years. Lou is a tad younger than me, and my favorite line when we are partners is, "GET IT, LOU."

Lou will tell you another favorite line of mine on the court is when neither one is playing up to snuff, I may mutter this: "WE CAN'T PLAY DEAD IN A COWBOY MOVIE!" You have to go back to the days of Roy Rogers and Gene Autry to understand that one.

I was very instrumental in Lou getting involved as a radio show host. Wimp didn't particularly like to come into the studio to do our show on Friday, preferring to do it by phone. After Lou retired, I asked him to join me in the studio on some Friday's. I later recommended him to a station in South Alabama, near his original home in Atmore. They hired him and he spent fourteen years, hosting a morning talk show.

The Barkley Story

It was the first part of October in 2020. The coronavirus was in full swing when Jan became violently ill. She was in serious condition for several weeks, but it wasn't from COVID. It appeared to be from a myriad of things, and her situation was touch and go until the doctors were able to get a handle on the cause of her illness.

While Jan was in the hospital, Charles Barkley traveled to Auburn to visit her. They spent the greater part of an hour together. Charles insisted on getting to know more about our family. Jan fill him in, while Charles sat there absorbing it like a sponge.

Two exciting things happened on the visit by Charles. All the nurses on Jan's floor wanted to get their picture made with him. He was accommodating them as best he could when the Supervisor of Nursing suggested they move to the end of the hall so that hospital business could continue as usual. Things had become a tad disruptive.

As Charles made his way down the hallway to the picture-taking session, he did something quite unusual. He stopped by each room along the hallway and shook hands with patients and visitors. It was a very heart-warming experience.

Jan was in the hospital for 40 days but made a remarkable recovery. She is home doing well as I write this.

I want to share with you one more situation involving Charles. I saw great potential in him as a basketball player when he came to Auburn. But he had a streak of laziness at times that affected his play. I must admit that I drove him hard to improve.

Fast forward to the unveiling of a statue in front of the new basketball arena at Auburn a few years ago. After I had given Charles an excellent introduction, he stood up and told the audience that he had been at Auburn for three months before he realized his name was not

SOB. This past year on national TV, he expressed that I was like a father to him. "I hated coach back then, but I love him like a father now," said Barkley. Thank you, Charles.

It's gratifying how many former players have had similar feelings. To me, this was the most rewarding thing about coaching –to see so many young boys grow into mature, productive men.

Well, it's time to move on to the main event. Before we do that, I want you to know that the people I have met, the friends I have made, the lives I have been able to touch all have helped make this a memorable and incredible journey. Let's go!! Are you ready for a great learning experience?

PART

II

Personal Readiness

Chapter Four

UP YOUR ATTITUDE

Probably nothing has been written about, talked about, and discussed more to the importance of success in athletics than has this mental state called attitude. Virtually every activity you engage in every day calls for thinking, choosing, and acting. Everything you think, every decision you make, every course of action you take, is influenced, either directly or indirectly, by your attitudes. In an authentic way, "You are your attitudes…and your attitudes are you."

"Okay," you might ask, "I see that this attitude thing is important, but what exactly is an attitude?" Our definition of attitude is that it is a predisposition to think positively or negatively about the circumstances, events, situations, and people you encounter every day.

After making these decisions over some time, it takes little conscious effort to decide how to react to the same stimuli in your environment going forward. In essence, you have created a habit. So, in the beginning, you form your attitudes, and those same attitudes develop habits. Then, in the end, both your attitudes and habits create you. Can you wrap your hands around that?

You can take this to the bank; athletic success begins with your overall attitudes--with what's inside of you--not what's around you. A key factor in your journey to be an elite athlete is to pay close attention to your attitudes because your attitudes will be the cause of most of the things that happen to you.

You cannot control everything that happens to you, but what you can control do it with a positive mindset. By creating this kind of mindset, things get better because you do everything in your power to make them better. You learn to adjust your attitudes to embrace settings that are favorable to making productive things happen and obtaining maximum results.

We want to backtrack a bit and ask you a question. Do you have a proper understanding of what being positive and optimistic means? We believe you can find the answer to that question by gaining insight into what situations in your athletic experience create negative thoughts and actions. Getting a handle on the negativity that arises from certain activities and events in your life is the starting place for dealing with them more positively and optimistically. As you monitor your self-talk, be vigilant in making corrections as you go. Replace that negative thought with a positive, uplifting viewpoint.

Upgrading your attitudes is a life-long task, one which requires almost infinite refinement. Unless you are vigilant and undergo constant awareness, you will not see where to make positive and optimistic adjustments. We will have more on this concept in the chapter SELF TALK MATTERS.

Positive thinking holds you in good stead in the world of athletics that is constantly throwing demanding challenges at you. It allows you to mitigate the negative effect that events or circumstances can have on success. Creating a mental picture of being an elite athlete trains your mind to expect and work at what it takes to be an elite athlete.

Performance Rule #1

On the quality of your attitudes, you rise,
If you are ever to receive the top prize;
For it is true the attitudes you possess,
Determines the level of your success.
So always remember your attitudes rule,
That in any situation, they become the tool
Which determine if you remain as you are,
Or move forward to perform like a real star.

-Source unknown

If You Believe…

If you believe you are beaten, you are;
If you believe you can't succeed, you don't;
If you want to achieve, but believe you can't;
Reality says it's almost a cinch you won't.
If you believe you'll fail, chances are you will;
For out in the athletic world, you will find
The route to success begins with your attitude --
Achievement rests in your state of mind.
If you believe you're outclassed, you are;
You have to believe in yourself to rise;
You have to believe you have what it takes,
If you are to regularly win the top prize.
The greatest successes don't always go
To the most talented woman or man;
For sooner or later, those who achieve,
Are those who really believe they can!!

-Adapted from unknown source

Elite athletes realize performing well can never be regarded as unplanned. Playing well is intentional. It is a direct reflection of the attitudes you have toward focusing on your role…on being responsible to do your job…to give your best effort every time. By sheer determination and willpower, you draw on your positive habits of thinking that make a significant difference in your play now, and as you develop your talents and abilities in the future.

"It isn't who you are…where you are…how you are…or what you are that leads to success…it is what you think about who you are."

-Bob Taylor

"Heart is Your Strongest Muscle."

"Excellence at anything requires a heart and soul effort... and you put your heart and soul into action when you perform as hard as you can…as well as you can...as determined as you can…as effective as you can."

-Woody Hayes

Everything else being about equal, probably the biggest differences between winning and losing is about a foot – which is roughly the difference from your head to your heart. Count on it: The 'why' in your heart will consistently mean more to building a better future than the 'how' in your head.

"There is apparently something that is not always equal during competitive events. Results are not always achieved by pitting strategy against strategy…strength against strength…skill against skill. More times than not, when there is competition involved, events are decided by an intangible factor known as heart."

-Marv Levy

No Heart…Little Chance

Others can measure how tall you are and how much you weigh;

They can measure the strength in your body and the level of your skills;

They can measure the depth of your knowledge and the height of your intelligence;

But they cannot measure the size of your heart...only you can measure that.

Wherever your heart is that's where your focus will be."

-Pat Head Summit

"The attitudes your heart creates dictates
the kind of success that you ultimately enjoy."

-Og Mandino

Things that dwell in the heart are
rarely curtailed by outside circumstances.

-Fritz Crisler

"If your heart is not in what you are doing, all the training in the world will not avail in the face of strong opposition. Fear drives out all memory of what it takes to resist and prevail, and renders knowledge useless."

-General Omar Bradley

"What is essential to success is invisible to the naked eye"

-Lou Carnesecca

Personal Attitudes Worth Having

- **"My success is by design."** A sense of the kind of athlete I want to be is crucial to becoming one. That's the reason I must have a plan for becoming an elite athlete. I realize that I rarely get more than I plan to get.
- **"I won't be embarrassed by my excitement for doing what's important to me."** I will think about letting my excitement for what I am doing bring others up to my level, not let their lack of excitement bring me down to their level.
- **"My 'why' will carry me a great deal further than my 'how'."** My abilities won't get me up and going, but desire will.

- **"What I might consider being no chance may well turn out to be my best chance."** I appreciate that my best chance for a successful athletic journey starts where I am right now.

- **"I understand every choice that I make carries a potential consequence."** I will think through all of the potential performance-enhancing choices I face and the possible repercussions…and then decide the very best route to take.

- **"I see myself as I can become -- not as I am."** I firmly believe my potential will continue to grow and develop. I recognize I have what it takes to be an elite athlete, starting right where I am... just as I am, and believe it with all I am!

- **"I will be straight up with myself."** What am I capable of doing with my present experience and skill set? Spend time and energy working hard to improve who you are right now. Then move confidently forward day by day.

- **"An attitude of curiosity will be my trademark."** A smart move on my part is to tackle the future with an attitude of "What's next? Bring it on." I see that as a winner's trademark.

- **"I will be a guiding light for others."** It is critical for me never to underestimate how my attitude can affect my teammates. My positive attitude may not make an impression on everyone, but it will make an impression on someone.

- **"I will always strive to leave things better than I found them."** When making things better is my constant companion, I will work hard toward improving all that I do.

- **"I understand that my personal athletic experience will expand or shrink according to my attitudes."** I will engrave that in my heart …because it is true.

- **"I will always remember that I make my attitudes, and my attitudes make me."** Enough said.

Elite athletes don't just see the possibility, they become the possibility.

"Those around you will be drawn to the optimistic attitude and enthusiasm you radiate on a consistent basis. They will desire to experience some of the excitement that you possess. They will want some of the glow and warmth that you bring to your daily activities, whether it be in practice or a game. That's what being positive does."

-Ray Tanner

"Staying positive does not mean that everything will turn out okay…rather it is knowing that you will be okay no matter how things turn out."

– Author unknown

Armed with an internal set of expectations that you can function at your best whatever the odds, those expectations alone will enhance your chances of becoming an (elite athlete).

Earl Nightingale

Attitude of Expectancy

- Expect the best from yourself, and more often than not, you will get it. Expect the best because you don't deserve anything less. You are worth the best that sports have to offer.
- If you expect good things to happen, you become more endowed with a particular attitude that creates conditions that make good things happen.
- Expecting to succeed minimizes the intimidation factor of almost any challenge.
- Having an internal set of expectations that you can win alone will enhance your chances of being a winners.
- By mentally participating in the expectant reality that something

- good is going to happen, will become the direction in which your efforts will take you.
- When you possess an attitude of positive expectancy, you make the waiting period between events a great deal more pleasant,
- Good things are more apt to come your way when you are expecting them.
- When you believe it is so before it becomes so, it has a better chance of being so.
- Your expectations can be focused on how you can succeed at what you are doing or focus on why you will fail. Either way, your prevailing attitude will contribute to making it a reality.
- Expect to achieve every time and watch your success ratio rise accordingly…there is magic in expectations.

Expecting the best does not make the road to winning any easier, but it does mentally increase the possibility. You perform with the exciting expectancy that your very best performance is just around the corner…and it is!

An Attitude of Gratitude

This is a brief expansion of our discussion of appreciation as one of our ten personal traits in Chapter Seven. Do you have an "attitude of gratitude?" The more you show your gratitude, the greater the chances you will connect with a brighter future. So be thankful for who you are…what you have… and where you are, for with that attitude you will make strides going forward.

No doubt, the feelings of gratitude you receive or those you express to others create an ever-increasing sense of well-being. If you feel and regularly express gratitude, you will tend to appreciate your health in a greater way. This leads to taking better care of yourself, and as a result, you feel more energetic and more prepared to perform.

"Achievement drives us, yet it's
gratitude that ultimately fulfills us."
--Roger Federer

"If you are not thankful for what you have now,
what makes you think you would be happy with more?"
-Mark Twain

The level of enjoyment you experience in sports--and in life--will be in many ways determined by what you scatter--not by what you gather.

A SONNY MOMENT

In order for an individual player to utilize his talent in achieving personal and team goals will to a greater extent depend on his state of mind. The ultimate benefit of a positive state of mind is that it is a powerful tool in helping you skillfully handle sports--and life. Your mindset is something that you always carry with you. It provides the basis of what you believe and the actual value of what you do. Without an optimistic mindset, a primary piece of the success puzzle is missing.

One fascinating thing about the right mindset is you always put a positive slant on any situation. This is big. When you approach your decisions and choices with an affirmative frame of mind, the force of this mindset moves you toward rather than moving you away—embracing rather than rejecting—the challenges before you. I guarantee that you cannot think negative thoughts and expect positive answers.

I have also found through the years that if a player possesses the inner quality of a positive mindset, then even if that player lacks exceptional talents and abilities, he can play a vital role on the team.

I believe that athletics calls for a state of mind that is stable and consistent. A state of mind that remains consistently constructive, despite ups and downs and normal fluctuations of play, helps a player emerge on the other side in much better shape—both mentally and on the scoreboard. With this perspective, it's easier to make the right decision because a player is always seeking to find a way for something good to happen. It is total immersion.

Do you need to overcome specific negative ways of thinking? Make a sustained effort to change external behavior which begins with changing underlying attitudes and feelings. This is an effort designed to act on your behalf and move the compass needle in your direction.

When you make positive behavior the centerpiece of your daily activities, you will eventually bring about genuine internal change. Your positive mindset will beget a positive response to outside stimuli. You will see things differently and react to them differently. This might be the most important effort you ever make in your entire sports career.

The way we behave, think, and feel is learned behavior. Being mindful of this should make you more vigilant in suspending negative thoughts and pessimistic reactions.

If creating and maintaining a positive mindset is a challenge for you, be aware that it may take a while to turn things around. Whatever steps, however small, you take towards learning to reduce the influence of negative attitudes will make a difference in everything you do. Negative thoughts are going to pop up on occasion, but you have a choice as to what you do with them.

Just keep in mind, how you respond to the action around you calls in large measure for exercising the sheer power of concentration. However, it serves little purpose unless you look at the positive side rather than the negative side of a situation. Participate mentally in the reality that something good will happen and it will, more often than not.

A positive mindset will help your self-confidence and create a more constructive approach as you tackle your responsibilities on the team. By way of a reminder, everything you do--time usage, approach to the game plan, preparation, practice, and execution--all are dependent on the quality of your mindset.

The ultimate benefit of a positive mindset is that it extends far beyond the playing field. It allows you to embrace all of life--to be fully alive and human. Beyond the world of athletics lies before you a bigger field to play on, and it's a game that an optimistic viewpoint will equip you to win…regardless of what you do.

Chapter Five

BELIEVE IN YOU

Am I where I am because that's where I want to be? If I am not where I want to be, then what is keeping me from moving where I am to where I want to be? Could it possibly be in the fact that I don't believe enough in me?

-Unknown young athlete

The "Right Stuff"

One of the greatest discoveries you can make is to fully understand your talents and abilities. That knowledge will determine what you can do. Yet it will be the attitude you hold toward yourself and your ability to perform that will determine how well you perform.

Once you embrace who you are, you have positioned yourself to visualize the athlete you can become realistically. Your mental process then flows in a constant state toward becoming that athlete.

There is little doubt that many who have gone on to greater heights in athletics have had to overcome some self-doubts about themselves. Most likely there were times when they had to wonder if they could meet and overcome all the challenges being faced as they traveled the path toward their athletic goals.

Essential during those times when they were not making progress is the fact they continuously took stock of themselves. They believed they had the right stuff to make it big in the world of sports. They believed that despite setbacks and temporary feelings of doubt, a renewed positiveness of their mindset would propel them forward toward more significant progress and greater possibilities.

These champions recognized that the most important thing they had to work with was what they possessed from the bottom of their feet to the top of their head. They had everything they needed within themselves, and it was up to them to ensure they never lost sight of that fact, even when faced with tough sledding.

Think on these words: Believing you have the "right stuff" will not create new talent and abilities. What this attitude toward yourself does is help you release, utilize and maximize your store of great talent and abilities.

"Nothing is impossible with you...
the word itself says 'I'm possible'."
-Aubrey Hepburn

State of Becoming

We can say without reservation that winning begins inside of you--not around you. As an inside-out proposition, you cannot always change what goes on around you, but you can change your thought patterns about what is happening around you. You cannot always create a different kind of environment, but you can make the best of the domain you are in. We have probably already said this, but we say it again with emphasis on its importance.

It starts by creating a mindset where things get better because you did something to make them better. You can invariably adjust your attitude to accommodate the kind of environment favorable to making strides in improving yourself.

When you create a mental picture of success, regardless of the conditions around you, you are training your mind to work at what it takes to be a winner. This begins with an internal set of expectations that you will make every effort to function at a peak level whatever the odds. Those expectations alone will lead to playing on a higher plane.

When you are not progressing as well, you would like to become the player you want to be, don't blame your shortcomings solely at the feet of talent and ability. How do you know the extent of your capabilities? You don't!

The barrier to becoming the very best athlete you possibly can become has little to do with your capabilities. It depends on the application you use in developing the abilities you possess. This is what keeps you evolving and improving.

What we are talking about is for you to reach the fulfillment of your desires depends on releasing more and more of the undiscovered potential locked inside of you. It is there, and your ability to unfold this potential is always in a state of becoming. So, visualize the athlete you can become—not the one you are. This will keep you from putting a limit on what you are capable of achieving. From this beginning, work hard every day to raise your level of play. No price is too great to pay. Remember the words of Yogi Berra: "Make the most of who you are…for that is all there is of you."

> "Consistency in performing any of your assigned tasks well can never be regarded as incidental or accidental. It will be a direct reflection of the attitude you have toward your ability to perform with a high level of consistency."
>
> -Author Unknown

The belief that you have what it takes to be an elite athlete will make up for a great many limitations in experience or capabilities you might have...but if you don't feel this way, regardless of how gifted or experienced you are, you won't be consistently successful when faced with sport's stiffest challenges.

"We either progress or regress…we don't stand still."
-Zig Ziglar

Do You Believe?

You are a more unique and special athlete than you have ever appreciated.

You have far more talent and ability than you have ever dared to imagine.

You have the capacity to grow beyond any performance level than you have ever performed.

You are much stronger and indeed more courageous than your inner fears have ever allowed you to be.

You are far more capable of dealing with difficult situations than you have ever thought possible.

You have more inner strength to handle tough setbacks and missteps than you have ever given yourself credit for.

You carry within you more greatness as an athlete than you have ever dreamed about.

You have been richly endowed by God with capabilities to move beyond what you are for the greater reward of what you can become.

Believe it with all your heart… because it is true.

UNFOLD POTENTIAL

Unfolding potential begins with focusing on your strengths, rather than on your limitations...on the reasons why you can succeed--not on what might hold you back. When you begin to believe that you can be the successful athlete your vision tells you can become, that's when you reach toward the future and do things you have dreamed of doing, things you might have thought in past that you could even possibly do.

Personal Brand

What is a personal brand? A personal brand originates in the depths of our being. It originates in our purpose for living and is expressed in our relationships and actions. Highly successful people find their purpose, build a brand based on it, and boldly express themselves through that brand. A personal brand permits the world to come to see the true, authentic you.

The key to why a personal brand works is that it allows others to know you personally. It lets you share what is unique about who you are and what you are capable of doing. It is based on what you stand for and what is important to you. It also let's those who connect with you better understand what you believe in and why you believe it. It serves to help others to bond with you on a broader personal basis.

A personal brand helps to definitively and consistently define and communicate who you are. It's the essence of what you want to achieve or experience in the world as you go forward.

Developing a Personal Brand

An authentic "personal brand" development focuses on three questions: What is your "**what**?" Your "**that**?" Your "**why**?" You may have settled on the answers to those three questions long ago. You might have answered them without consciously realizing it. But if you really haven't gotten around to finding the answers or have never even thought about these types of questions, take the time to do so now.

Steve Olsher was a guest on my (Lou) radio show several times. Steve wrote a best seller entitled: "What is Your What?" Steve defines our "what" as our entire being from the top of our heads to the bottom of our feet. Our "what" are the talents and abilities we bring to the table.

Next up is your "that?" When you say, "I am good at "that'," or "I enjoy doing 'that," what do you mean? The design of a personal brand is primarily built around the answers to those questions. Formulate a simple, short statement to let others know the essence of your "that." It will help improve your focus.

Now comes the big question of "why?" "Why" is what keeps desire high and provides the inner drive to keep us going when conditions are tough.

After you have written down a statement that describes your "what" and your "that", write down ten "whys" that describe why you want to be an elite athlete. Think in terms of the four facets that factor into being an elite athlete: Body, brain, heart, and soul. Do you have a good "why" in each of these areas that will highlight your "what," and primarily your "that?"

Compare two young athletes with the same goals and similar abilities. One becomes an outstanding athlete, while the other experiences little success at all. Why? The answer in many cases is found in the "why." All things being equal, the young athlete who enjoys a higher level of athletic success does so because he has more "why" than the athlete who has limited success.

Your "what" and your "that" are important. But if you want to achieve something great in the athletic world, get crystal clear on your "why." Your "why" will guide you through the bumps and bruises of sports and help you emerge on the other side as an elite athlete. Take the time to write down at least ten "why's" of what you would like to accomplish as an athlete.

Your personal brand will strengthen your outlook and your confidence in yourself. The key element is to understand that it all begins with answering the three questions we asked earlier: What is your "what?" Your "that?" Your "why?" We suggest you do this before reading any further.

Having a positive attitude about your own potential is an absolute necessity to establishing a pattern of success. Out of all the possibilities available to you in any situation, you are going to select that which is consistent with the kind of performer you see yourself being. Without exception you will perform the way you believe you can. No more. No less.

A Touch of Realism

"You can do and be what you want to do and be…in time." We believe that. We trust you do as well.

You have probably already experienced a touch of realism that you cannot reach a stage of expertise overnight. Prowess in athletics is developed over time after much trial and success. While it is important to look down the road at the athlete you would like to be, it is equally important to look at what you can do right now.

Simply put, undeveloped abilities, resources, and experience generally tighten a clamp around your present performance level. While developmental factors limit the extent of how quickly you can satisfy your athletic dreams and desires, the most influential limit is not what you have...it is how you go about using what you have.

The best rule to follow is to be explicit about who you are and we you are in your athletic developmental phase. Admittedly, there is the tendency to get in over your heads by undertaking more than you can capably do at this point. Expecting too much too soon tends to erode confidence and thwart your athletic development.

What do you hear us saying? How about not letting fear and self-doubt in your abilities grow because you expected to make incredible strides right off the bat. Making steady progress is the key to being the very best player you can be. Growth is in increments and plateaus. That's how you make progress. That's reality.

> "Ability is a gift and a challenge. It is something you use not just something you have…and the more of your ability that you use, the more you realize you have available to use."
>
> -William Danforth

A SONNY MOMENT

I once had a team that was dramatically underperforming. A sports writer ask me, "What's the matter with your team?" Without giving my answer much thought, I responded: "What's wrong with this team can be summed up in one word, selfishness." Be darn if I wasn't right.

Through all my years of coaching I had players with an exaggerated sense of their own abilities and what they could accomplish. These players were driven by the desire to showcase their egos, mostly to their own detriment and subsequently the team's. It has been my experience that as egos grow, so does conceit and arrogance generally leading to negative consequences for the development of quality team chemistry.

The thing most peculiar to the selfish athlete is that his motivation is in being the "go to person," who is motivated solely by his own desire to be on the highlight reel. Unfortunately, the selfish athlete has a tendency to feel that he is above any coaching or constructive criticism. I can guarantee that when I was coaching, a player with substance instead of style was the one in the game when it is on the line.

I have found there is a distinct line between being a self-confident team player and being a selfish, cocky player. Cockiness indicates the lack of maturity that comes from being unsure of one's level of confidence. In this regard, a player tends to act the part, but come crunch time he fails to perform the part. That player, in many cases has not demonstrated the capabilities of being the "phenom" he thinks he is.

No player can be great if he is moved by selfishness and not by desire for the common good. Those players who are so absorbed with themselves and their own affairs, fail to contribute to the overall good of the team. It is difficult to preserve a sense of team unity, which is essential to winning, to have players who think only of themselves.

The more selfish a player is, the more easily can a desire for personal accolades lead him to acts that hurts the overall effort of the team. Players with an inflated sense of self-worth in fact can be a cancer on a team. They need to understand that if they cannot be a functional part of the team, there can occupy either of two spots: a place at the end of the bench or in the bleachers.

On the other hand, a self-confident player creates things that have more positive consequences. The talented, self-confident player who enjoys the whole experience of team play, in my estimation, is more apt to achieve fame and wide renown. He is not seeking to be the lead story on the sports pages, but has a really good chance of ending up there.

Any athlete who approaches teammates with a self-reliant point of view puts himself in a position where no other teammate is in a position higher than his own. Therefore, he has no reason to be envious or seek greater attention than his teammates. Since he has no need to prove himself to anyone or to show off his personal superiority in order to win praise or admiration, he is free of any struggle for dominance.

I don't care how good of an athlete you are, forego any idea that you are better or more important than any other team member. In teamwork, there is no above or below, no in or out, everyone associated with the team is in it together.

Before I go, I would like to place emphasis on the importance of togetherness. In sport and in life, your security, your happiness, your success is never yours alone. The greatest source of strength you will ever have is found in your relationships. On a team that means everyone relies on the actions and functions of each other.

In sports, each teammates' role and responsibility is most often distinct and specialized. Yet, reliance on each other is what makes it a team. A key factor in this reliance is trust. I believe trust is what empowers teammates to meld together to and get the job done. There is a built-in connection that goes beyond X's and O's. Players and coaches alike trust each other to do their part—and do it well. Embrace trust. It is the secret to togetherness. Let me leave you with this quote:

The TV cameras don't show up for just
anybody…so don't be just anybody."
-Ray Perkins

Chapter Six

SELF TALK MATTERS

"If you believe, talk and act like a winner,
you have an excellent chance of being a winner;
If you believe, talk and act like a loser,
you have an excellent chance of being a loser."
-Source unknown

Have you ever thought about how much you talk to yourself? We all have some self-generated dialogue taking place privately in our minds during our waking hours. What are you telling yourself about yourself? The reality of self-talk is that it can make you…or break you.

Dr. Frank Allen reminds us. "Your self-talk has brought you to where you are, and it most surely will carry you to where you want to go in sports...and in life. You are, and can be, nothing more than the total results of what you tell yourself you are--and can be at any point or any place in time."

Before we continue, pause here and answer a few questions: Are you primarily telling yourself what is wrong with you, rather than what is right with you? Do you tend to remind yourself about what you cannot do, rather than what you can do? Do you dwell on your "minus" powers, rather than on your "plus" powers? Do you use your energy to put yourself down, rather than build yourself up? Do you consistently talk to yourself about yourself in a negative way?

Privately, are you saying to yourself, "I'm not good at this…" or "I'm not good at that? The truth behind the answers to these questions is the more you look at the negative side of yourself, your reality will reflect this negative image.

Unfortunately, speaking negatively to one's self is a widespread habit. More often than not, we can be our harshest critic. It may not happen often, but our experience is that there is a tendency to be more cynical toward ourselves than conditions would warrant.

Another factor that works against you when you talk yourself "down" is keeping your faults and flaws front and center in your mind. In this manner, your self-talk has a way of becoming a self-fulfilling prophecy. Each time you are negative to yourself, you take a step forward in getting good at being bad to yourself.

Now you might say, "I don't mean these things I am saying to myself about myself," or "What difference does it make, you might ask? I rarely mean it when I say negative things about myself." Seldom do we really "mean" the negative things we say about ourselves. But isn't there an inherent problem here? Tell that to your subconscious mind. It doesn't know the difference. It works on the GIGO theory: "Good in, good out," or "Garbage in, garbage out."

Without the support of your positive self-talk, it is tough to perform at a high level. Action on the outside consistently follows the action on the inside. You probably innately know that, but it is easy to underestimate the power self-talk has on personal success continually. Is this something you need to work on going forward?

Anything we do results from what we think, and what we think is influenced mainly by what we are telling ourselves about our capacity. That's the bottom line.

So, the first lesson paramount to developing and building an elite athletic status rests upon the most straightforward strategy. It is a strategy that if you stick with it, using it over and over, you are almost sure to succeed. This simple strategy is to consistently speak the language of success to yourself about yourself. Talk yourself up!

Positive, upbeat language spoken persistent enough to yourself will eventually become a part of your belief system. Just remember, be careful what you say to yourself, because someone very important is listening…and that is you.

Monitor Your Self-Talk

This area of monitoring self-talk requires applying as much mental muscle as you may produce humanly. It is that important. Improved self-talk begins with monitoring your self-talk. While it takes a lot of focus and discipline to change old self-talk patterns and attitudes, it may just hold the key to your taking a big step toward a brighter future.

Changing your self-talk habits begins with being very aware of how you are speaking to yourself, notably when facing a tense or stressful situation. Being aware of what you are saying to yourself about yourself in these situations is the beginning of the process of refining self-talk. Once you have taken this vital first step, you will find yourself continuously working to improve your self-talk patterns.

In this process, you are working toward two very different goals. First, learn what situations create a tendency for you to trigger negative comments. Ask yourself, "What am I telling myself about this particular situation that is negative and self-defeating?"

Second, effectively change your inner dialogue to seek a more positive and upbeat direction. A great tool to use here is the *"Take two"* technique used in making movies. When you do slip up and talk negatively about yourself, you simply back up and strike it from the record and silently say, *"Take two"*—and begin anew.

Fueled by the thrust of this positive approach, you begin to make strides in improving your self-talk…and your performance. You may feel a bit strange or uncomfortable talking to yourself in a novel manner, primarily because of the subconscious mind. All this new, positive, upbeat self-talk will give the old programming in your subconscious mind quite a shock. The subconscious is not accustomed to all those wonderful new descriptions you are using in describing yourself. It will question if you really mean them. But it can learn…if you stay with it.

Any way you look at it, when you talk in a positive, upbeat way to yourself about yourself continually and consistently, everything you do will move toward the positive side. Your self-talk is a powerful force…use it to your advantage.

So, here is our suggestion: For the next twenty-one days, consciously focus on speaking the language of success to yourself. A vital objective should be one where you strive to eliminate those inaccurate and unrealistic inner conversations as they crop up and immediately replace them with something more positive and upbeat. From this base, you can challenge those erroneous assumptions and beliefs you have told yourself over time. This puts you in a position to follow the new and more accurate inner messages lead.

Self-Talk Guidelines

Try these self-talk guidelines on for size. They will fit:

- Work to eliminate your "apostrophe tees." Can't, won't, shouldn't do, wouldn't do, and don't want to, all do nothing to elevate you to a higher performance level. The less these "apostrophe tees" are used, the more the focus is on positives…not on negatives.

- Get off your "buts." Much too often, "Yes, but…" becomes the hallmark of too many aspiring athletes. The problem with "Yes, but" is that everything that comes before the "but" has little to no meaning. The real nugget of what you want to say comes after the but. The smart move: Get off your "buts" so you can get more of the positive things done.

- Learn to use the "in the bag" concept. Whatever you want to change or improve, state it in the present tense as an accomplished fact. Make self-talk statements like: "I am...", "I have..." "I do..."

Untie Your "Nots"

It's a big deal when aspiring athletes tie themselves in "nots." To use self-defeating statements like: "I'm not good at this..." or "I'm not good at that…" can easily lead to a self-fulfilling prophecy.

Successful athletes through the ages learned the importance of "untying the nots" in their lives:

The have nots…
The can nots…
The do nots…
The will nots…
The may nots…
The could nots…
The would nots…
The should nots…
The am nots…

Especially the "am nots." For example, "I am not good enough." Sure, you are…if you believe it.

You are what you tell yourself you are;
You do what you tell yourself you can do;
You become what you tell yourself you can become;
You generally get what you tell yourself you deserve.
-Source unknown

Listen to Your Heart

"There is always a 'doomsayer' around who is going to tell you that you can't do something or there's no reason to try. But you don't have to take it to heart and begin telling yourself that's it true. It will never be the truth unless you do something to make it that way."

-Bobby Dodd

One of the biggest challenges facing young athletes is hearing those who are part of their inner-circle suggest that they are incapable of doing something. "What makes you think you can be successful at that?" This is a theme well-meaning parents and friends lay on aspiring athletes. As the famous philosopher Yogi Berra once said, "Others can tell you that you can't do it, but that doesn't always work."

Yogi is right: Why would you buy into the words of those who would rob you of your future aspirations? Their comments can only affect you if you allow them. It is within your power to determine what outside forces will have a chance to influence your future.

Whatever you do, don't let a dream stealer rob you of your dream to be something special. When you make the decision that you want to be extraordinary, go after it with all your heart -- or else someone is apt to sell you a bill of goods that you can't make it…that you can't be highly successful. Ask yourself, just how successful has that person been?

Make your definition of who you are and what you can achieve – then do your dead level best to move beyond any negative comments. Always listen to your heart. That's your best self talking to you.

Spend little time with people who are a haven for negative thoughts and harmful actions. You put yourself in a loser's position when you associate with those who regularly say: *"It can't be done, why try?"* It is wise to remember: Those who fail to increase you will eventually decrease you…those who fail to make you better will eventually make you worse.

Hang Out with Those Who…

· give you a bigger concept of yourself…

· are constantly encouraging you…

· perform the way you want to perform…

· bring out your best qualities when in their presence.

A SONNY MOMENT

One of the biggest issues in my estimation on this self-talk subject is the player who has the tendency to lie to himself. It is challenging for some athletes to undertake a reality check and accept where they stand in their athletic quest.

Whatever you do, don't lie to yourself. If you have failed up to this point in fulfilling your dreams and aspirations, who should you blame? If you are not where you had hoped to be and have not reached your established goals, whose fault is that?

Can you blame your lack of progress on circumstances? Who ultimately makes the choices that alter who you are and where you are going? Can you place the blame on others? Do you honestly believe other people have more influence on your decisions than you do? Or, is the barrier to becoming the athlete you want to be looking back at you in the mirror?

Although your environment does play a role in achieving success, you do not have to be at the mercy of environmental circumstances. On the contrary, you can deliberately choose to make the best of wherever you find yourself. Therefore, don't blame the lack of progress solely on the conditions around you. Regardless of external influences, you hold the power to make the best of where you are and what you are doing. Change your self-talk.

Your self-talk is the starting point for improving what you want to become. If you embrace where you are in your development right now, you have positioned yourself to ultimately visualize the first step in what you want to be as an athlete. If you continually focus on your present state only, there will be little change.

On the other hand, if you routinely talk to yourself about the athlete you want to become and all the great attributes you possess, that's the direction your mental activities will carry you. Then it will be only a matter of time until you are making great strides toward becoming an elite athlete. The law of attraction is a potent force. That's the power of your positive self-talk.

Chapter Seven

WINNING TRAITS

It is our conviction that reaching elite athletic status depends significantly on the developmental level of certain personal traits. We feel very strongly certain personal traits can make a significant difference in the success you experience on your athletic journey.

It is true that when adequately developed by young athletes, personal traits can add immensely to incremental improvement both at and away from the athletic arena. We mean that you don't have to stop and ask themselves how am I supposed to react to this situation. Instead, when you are grounded by quality personal traits, you naturally react positively because those traits sit right at the heart of who you are.

There are countless personal traits that we could select from, so how did we go about selecting the ones we highlight in this chapter? We believe words like necessary, needed, required, essential, vital, mandatory, indispensable…are how we look at the personal traits we will explore in this chapter. Of course, we are not saying these traits are written in stone, but young athletes who employ them in their daily athletic activities add proper stability and backbone to what they do.

There are two important points we want to mention before we look at our list of personal traits. First, personal traits are not easy to fake. They are either a part of you, or they are not. Neither can they be called up instantaneously to fit the whim of the moment. Their effectiveness is built on how they stand up over time.

Our second point is the effectiveness of personal traits in the interactions with others depends on the output. In other words, did your input produce the outcome you wanted? The litmus test for unique traits is this: Did repetitive conscious action on your part change the nature of how you reacted to given real-life situations? Did it change how you acted when undertaking challenges that mattered?

We can hear someone in the bleachers asking, "What do personal traits have to do with winning the 'head' game?" We believe a lot. Athletics starts with the body, but ultimately, the nature of the mind--the substance of your mindset--speaks to the level of achievement you experience in sports.

Many of these personal traits are already part of your make-up-- to varying degrees. The thrust of our discussion on these personal traits is to move you full fledge across the board in their development. Our desire for you is to possess a fully functional and workable platform for dealing with whatever sports throws your way. A solid toolbox of quality personal traits ultimately will lead you to meet and overcome an infinite variety of problematic tests in sports—and in life.

Deep down in the depths of your very being is the foundation for using sports as a stepping stone to a quality life. You may not end up being an elite athlete, but we guarantee you sports will help you build on the kind of personal traits that will enable you to tackle the world of work on your terms. In addition, the quality personal traits you sharpen through sports participation can arm you with the strength and courage to make great strides in your quest of becoming a great person.

This is the challenge before you. Read through the chapter. Then determine the personal trait you believe will create the most prominent transformation in moving your sports career forward. Consciously create a mental picture of what you need to concentrate on to ensure you maximize your growth in the personal trait, or traits, chosen. Ask yourself, what can I do to provide added confidence and energy to making this unique trait(s) a genuine part of my athletic life?

Here are the ten personal traits we have identified from years of experience as highly effective in developing elite athletic status. These personal traits offer a straightforward, confident approach to initiating great strides in the three areas which affect athletic participation—mental, physical, and emotional. Armed with the kind of energy and power offered by the many strategies and truisms offered in this book, your growth in personal traits will produce a new (or renewed) emphasis on what it will take to expand your horizons and experience greater growth as an athlete—and as a person.

We will now cover the ten specific personal traits you need to possess in your toolbox as you move headlong toward a successful athletic career. They are in no particular order of importance.

1. Positive Thinking
2. Self-Confidence
3. Mental Toughness
4. Pressure Tolerance
5. Self-Discipline
6. Adaptability
7. Integrity
8. Poise
9. Appreciation
10. Consistency

Positive Thinking

Little can stop you with a positive attitude,
little can help you with a negative attitude.

We touched on this in Chapter Four; positivity serves as the base for building a bright future. Converting your desire to be an elite athlete into reality depends significantly on how you employ positive thinking habits. For better or worse, these habits have led to your present level of play and will be the driving force behind your future play.

If you are not playing up to the level you would like and wish to change; any change will come as a result of a change in your thinking habits. Think of it this way: you consciously create your thinking habits, and then those same habits of thinking determine your future.

Over 50,000 thoughts pass through your mind daily–but you can only think one thought at a time. The task before you every moment is to control that single thought and think about the good in the situation, not the negative—about what can go right—not wrong.

Study after study has shown that athletes who have optimistic thinking habits experience more and broader successful outcomes than their more negatively thinking counterparts. They are healthier, have more energy, make better decisions, perform better, are less stressed, and more productive overall than pessimists.

However, there has been a lot of misunderstanding about creating and maintaining a positive mindset. It takes a lot more than repeating many feel-good one-liners (even though they help) to make positive thinking work in your life. It takes a proper understanding of what being optimistic means. Finally, it is being consciously aware, moment-by-moment, of what you are thinking.

We humans have the innate ability to adjust and change our thought patterns. We can train our minds to view events in our lives with a optimistic slant. It may take time for this to emerge, but life's trajectory can eventually be pointed toward the positive side. This is the side that will hold you in excellent stead in a sports world that is constantly throwing complex challenges at you. Furthermore, an optimistic viewpoint allows you to mitigate the negative effect of a tragic event.

Nowhere is the significance of this kind of mindset more prevalent than in a tense, competitive athletic event where being positive is so important. Your positive train of thought works best when you hone in on the activity and keep your focus on what is going on at any moment in time. This concentrated effort keeps you ready to consistently perform at a top-notch level, regardless of the nature of the action.

"The simplicity of thinking in a positive manner is that it demonstrates to others the joy of participating that resides within you. You don't need to wear a sign telling others how you feel on the inside. "They see it. They feel it. They know it." The words of Napoleon Hill.

Unleash the innate possibilities you possess. Your habits of thinking are what will initiate the steps that lead you there.

Self-Confidence

Sometimes the most challenging part of the journey is accepting the fact you are worthy of the trip.

Many talented athletes fail to measure up to their potential because of a lack of self-confidence. The significant factors interfering with self-confidence are low self-esteem, fundamental insecurity, an inferiority complex, or simple overall self-doubt.

Often at the base of this self-doubt in athletes is being told early in life they are not good enough or somehow incapable of being successful in athletics or anything else. Is this a challenge for you? Don't you dare, for one more second, believe the comments of others who are not aware of the greatness that you possess. In Chapter Four, we talked about how many of these comments come from those closes to us because they don't want to see us get hurt if we fail. We both understand this very well. We had overcome negativism around us to move on.

Building a bright future is dependent on possessing self-confidence par excellence. The remarkable capabilities that you have will grow as your self-confidence grows. Therefore, conquer this self-confidence quest to set the stage for fulfilling your potential as an athlete. It is no secret that how you view yourself will play a crucial role in your future.

Chapter Six highlights the importance of how self-talk makes a big difference in raising your self-image and the level of your self-confidence. If you tend to look at the "negatives" about yourself at the expense of your many "positive" qualities, the points below should be of great interest to you in building your self-confidence:

Be prepared. Knowledge management is crucial to developing self-confidence. The more you know, the more comfortable you feel in performing what you know. The reality is you will ultimately do what you are prepared to do.

Develop a growth mindset. A great way to get out of a self-deprecating and low self-esteem loop is to think about where you are headed, not where you have been. Focus on what you will do to make progress today.

Be excited about what you do. Being fired up about tackling the tasks and challenges you face is a vital step along the route to building self-confidence. They give you a chance to get better.

Stay active. You cannot acquire self-confidence sitting around waiting for something to happen. You must be actively involved to develop skills and improve overall abilities and expand your confidence level in the process.

Speak the winners' language. Talk to yourself like a winner. The positive affirmations that you tell yourself are vital to both self-confidence and longevity. Be a self-coach, not a self-critic.

Conduct mental rehearsals. Visualize in your mind's eye what you will do today to make positive things happen. When you conduct mental trials and follow them up with responsive action, the results can dramatically enhance your self-confidence.

Expect the best. When you participate mentally in the conviction that something good will happen today, that is the direction your confidence level will take.

Exercise patience. A deep and abiding confidence in yourself is something that takes time. It must be coaxed in step-by-step. In the end, what you earn will be the result of short, consistent gains.

Act the part. Act the role until you feel comfortable playing the role. Be a beacon of confidence around others. There is nothing more enlightening to others than letting your light shine so brightly that they will want to do the same.

Associate with winners. Spend little time with those who are a haven for negative thoughts. You gain self-confidence by associating with those who encourage you…who see you as being worthy of tackling your most formidable challenge…who appreciate that you have what it takes to make it big in the world of athletics.

Celebrate your successes. No matter how small or insignificant it may seem at the time. It is okay to pat yourself on the back—if you do something worthy. Use your successes to build on to develop the confidence to stretch out toward future success.

Don't wait until everything is just right. It will never be perfect. There will always be challenges, obstacles, and less-than-ideal conditions. So what? Just keep going. With each step you take, you will grow stronger and stronger, more and more skilled, more and more self-confident, and more and more successful in dealing with all kinds of situations and environments.

Mental Toughness

"When the going gets tough, the tough get going."

"Where there's a will there is a way."

"Never, never give in."

Heard any of these before? If you have been around the sports world for any length of time, we guarantee that you have. Without a doubt, these statements are factual. Tenacious people tend to win.

The question here is not about physical toughness. That is earned through preparation, practice, and hard work. The answer here is in the development of mental toughness. There is no light switch to flip to turn on your mental toughness. Physicality helps, but mental toughness is rooted deeper in yourself. It is very personal. It is more of a heart thing than a mind thing.

One of the givens of athletics is circumstances can change on a dime. Challenges have a way of popping up with regularity. If it were not for the challenges you face, the pitfalls you encounter, and the obstacles to overcome, how do you find out just how good you can be?

A shortcoming in developing mental toughness is the inability to recognize and appreciate that obstacles and difficulties are the only way to grow in personal responsibility. There is no sport where you can achieve a significant measure of success without encountering and overcoming adverse or challenging situations.

The elements of success are found in your ability to develop mental toughness that is readily available when those demanding situations arise. Of course, that might require a shift in habits. It might require that you rewire and retool the way you think. You may even need to see differently. But you are up for it, aren't you?

The gift of mental toughness is that there is no reasonable obstacle you cannot overcome and stay on the course to achieving a goal. In essence, where others see dangerous obstacles in their path, you see opportunity. Sounds like you, doesn't it?

Toughness is in your soul and spirit, not in your muscles.

Pressure Tolerance

When right on the brink of making a critical decision or executing a play in a crucial game situation, some athletes flinch… retreat…lose courage at the very moment it is most needed. Why? Our experience is the perception of a critical point in a game is inherently altered by one of the most notable opiates known to athletes: pressure.

How good are you at handling so-call "pressure situations?" How do you react amid stressful circumstances? Does your heart begin to pound more than usual? Do your palms become sweaty? Does a big lump develop in your throat? Do you have doubts you can meet the stressful situation head-on and create the outcome you desire? Those experience athletes who can handle crucial game conditions that have been labeled as "pressure situations" are the ones who have a leg up on elite status.

A truism of "pressure situations" is that they can either bring out the best in you–or the worst-- depending on how you view the situation, and ultimately, how you handle it. When released inwardly, it tends to have a harmful impact on performance by producing distinct physiological changes in the body.

The stress created in "pressure situations," if turned inwardly, limit's reaction time. Blood vessels constrict, which reduces blood supply to the brain affecting the ability to think clearly. The results are predictable: performance is less than it could be otherwise.

There is a brighter side to the stress produced by pressure...it doesn't always have to be negative. It can be a real positive force. Those so call "pressure situations" can bring greater depth and meaning to your play. This may vary from task to task…from game situation to game situation, depending on what you are facing. But we assure you that you can effectively handle the pressurized moments in sports by internalizing the following important lessons:

- The first contest of the season is just as important as the last.
- One game is never more critical than another game.
- One play is never more essential than another play.
- Focus on what you have been trained to do on every play, in every situation; then no one situation is ever more critical than the next--they are all critical.
- There are no pressure situations…only situations where participants feel or experience pressure.

The word pressure is tossed around a lot—it is a natural part of the sports vernacular--but in your mind in the future, everything that happens during play carries the same weight. Your goal is to embrace where you are and visualize performing optimally what you are expected to do. This is the best way for those so-called "pressure situations" to have minimal control over your affairs. It simply depends on how you go about managing it through your ability to exercise pressure tolerance.

"Pressure is a privilege…(elite athletes) learn to deal with it."
-Novak Djokovic

Self-Discipline

The depths of your self-discipline will gauge the height of your athletic success. It is the foundation on which you will turn your talents into quality performing attributes.

When you are told you need to be more disciplined, what does that mean to you? We would venture to say for athletic purposes; discipline is the bridge between the role you are asked to play and your ability to keep your focus on playing that role. We believe that discipline holds the key to the innate ability to focus on executing the task you are performing--not on what the execution result might mean. In essence, your concentration is on the “How to.” This generally leads to a much more satisfying conclusion.

The execution of a task is more powerful when you have a built-in ability to focus that is permanently maintained on a task, not one where the focus is attained now and then. In other words, a steady, disciplined approach will always exceed a wavering one.

What kind of mental discipline do you possess when you approach a difficult task or a crucial situation? Do you focus on what can go right? Or is your attention geared predominantly to what might go wrong?

When you discipline yourself to only think about the things you should be doing, the things you want to go right, your actions will reflect this positive approach. The odds will be in your favour for success when you keep your eyes on what you should be doing to execute your assignments. The role you are being trained to perform will become easier to perform.

Conversely, when you consistently think about what you shouldn't do, rather than what you should do, where is your mental focus? Aren't you intuitively tuning in to the "don'ts instead of the "dos" -- the negatives instead of the positives?

To avoid a negative "keep from failing" attitude, you simply need to discipline yourself to refrain from thinking about the negatives that can hold you back. A disciplined approach that emphasizes the positive –what you can do–will most likely direct your performances in a way that makes your intended outcome a successful reality.

Which is more indicative of you? Is this an area in your mindset toolbox that you need to take a serious look at? Occasionally, it is essential to check your focus. Ask yourself questions like: "Am I disciplined enough to focus on what I can do rather than what I cannot do? Am I disciplined enough to focus on what can go right rather than on what might go wrong? Am I disciplined enough to focus on what it takes to succeed, focused on what it takes to just keep from failing?"

"Winners love the discipline of hard work…it's the trade-off they are making to win. Losers, on the other hand, see hard work as a form of punishment. That's the difference."

–Lou Holtz

When you are winning, discipline yourself to perform as if you were behind.

"We need a disciplined mindset to do today what our opponents won't, so the next game we can accomplish what they can't."

– Dwayne' The Rock' Johnson

Adaptability

Sports is characterized by sudden, unexpected, and sometimes dramatic challenges. The aptitude to effectively rise to meet these challenges is a crucial element in almost any sport. A knack for making quick and decisive decisions can often be the slight difference that can make a big difference in your results.

The ability to function in a rapidly changing environment requires developing a flexible, malleable ability to adapt. An adaptive mindset is a conditioned mind that has been systematically trained, focused, concentrated, and tempered to reconcile and cope with immediate external changes. Adaptive thinking helps you to apply sound reasoning in recognizing and perceiving the actual reality of play, quickly and more correctly.

Armed with adaptability, you can maintain composure even in the most competitive and pressure-filled situations. It is through an adaptive mindset you learn to avoid extremes and overreactions. Adapting quickly and efficiently minimizes the emotional surges during actual gam action and gives you a stable power source.

Adaptability is a learned behavior. It is an essential factor in your ability to move your future forward. Most of us "old heads" realize any variation in behavior that challenges a core belief, or is incompatible with how we have been doing things, is not always easy to pull off.

Letting go is never easy. Altering the way we are doing things requires the highest level of adaptability. Yet, the younger you are, the quicker you can get into a groove of adaptive behavior.

Sometimes the "old ways" are the only ways you know because that's what you were taught. As the coaching around you improves, you must be ready to "let go" so you can create room for something better. One of the most challenging things for most of us to do is to detach ourselves from those things that feel "comfortable," to expand our experience and knowledge base. Take a moment to think about some of the ways you need to adapt in your quest to be an elite athlete.

How you approach changing your "old ways" makes all the difference in whether you do it successfully, or not. We are talking about creating an adaptive mindset where things get better because you have the fortitude and drive to discover how to make them better. This is the mindset that leads you to be deeply committed to establishing a highly productive path to being a quality athlete.

A clear fact when the intent is to adapt to new and more constructive ways of doing things is that you never let go entirely of the past. There will always be something of the past left within you. Every new beginning carries with it a lesson from things you have done previously in your life. Just realize that there is always something worthy from the past that makes the present adaptation easier.

Do you believe there is something better out there than you have ever experienced? If the answer is "Yes," then you have to adapt and do something differently, and you have to do it deliberately. It works best to be proactive from the insight that enables you to be reactive to needed adjustments. Armed with this kind of foresight, you can develop an arsenal of diverse strategies and tactics that will help you unlock the door to future athletic growth.

Integrity

You are what you are when no one is looking.

What does integrity mean to you? To us, integrity is an unrelenting demand to do your best every time within the confines of the rules. It cannot be achieved in short bursts of doing the right thing to satisfy the moment's impulse. It is doing what is ethically right—all the time. In other words, do what's right because it is right.

One of the most demanding forms of mental toughness is to make decisions you can live with tomorrow, not on what you might get away with today. Athletic participation calls for constant vigilance. It depends heavily on a mentality that is tuned to integrity.

To the very end, you are the total of your decisions and actions. Integrity cannot be counterfeited. It cannot be put on and taken off like a garment. Integrity is like the markings ingrained in the very heart of a tree—it is made evident by what you indeed are on the inside.

The marvel of integrity is it can be developed and nurtured. Begin with a clear picture of being the kind of athlete who is filled with integrity. As a person of integrity, you always enjoy the morally worthy satisfaction of having acted correctly. And that is the principle upon which sportsmanship rests.

We are going to take an in-depth look at the role integrity plays in sportsmanship in Chapter Twelve.

Be consistent and uncompromising any time there is a question of right and wrong.

Poise

Do reason and sound judgment play the dominant role in how you conduct your daily emotional affairs? You can be assured almost all the things you do in athletics are interpreted at the emotional level. In a natural way, you see and do things through the eyes of your emotions.

One of the more impressive things about elite athletes is their poise—the ability to balance reason with emotion. While they experience the depth and breadth of emotions, they have learned how to be balanced in dealing with situations that tend to produce heightened emotions. They display an element of consistency that creates balance.

It is essential to control impulses and act responsibly in emotional situations. The ability to experience the whole range of human emotions at the right time and in the right degree will dramatically impact your performance in a positive way.

This doesn't mean you will always refrain from having "negative emotional moments." What it does mean is you will experience them differently. You won't let them take over, nor will you dwell on them. You simply face them, make the necessary corrections and then move on to more constructive feelings.

What we hope you hear us saying is that top performers do not get too over-charged. They have a calmness and easiness about themselves that keep their equilibrium in pressure-cooker type situations that can arise in sports. They demonstrate poise and exercise composure in those situations where constraint is vital to high performance.

Stay within yourself. Others cannot make you lose emotional control; only you can do that to yourself.

Appreciation

We hope you are ready for this one. Do you believe offering and receiving words of appreciation makes for a healthier brain and body? It is true, the feelings of gratitude we experience and express to others create an ever-increasing sense of well-being. Studies have proven that appreciation and gratefulness enhance health.

When you feel thankful and regularly express gratitude, you tend to appreciate your health more. This leads to taking better care of yourself, and as a result, you feel more energetic and fuller of life. Gratitude helps sustain a high-energy thought pattern that connects you to the best that's around you. Your appreciative mind will focus on that best, and therefore you will attract the best.

Possessing an "Attitude of Gratitude" helps you to be more resilient, too. By being constantly aware of the thoughtful acts of others, you tend to look for the positive in almost any situation. This makes it easier for you to overcome the trauma of any kind of bad experience.

Are you mindful enough to reflect upon your present blessings and are grateful for what you have? You have received a ton of blessings to be thankful for--and the more you focus on them and not on your past misfortunes—we guarantee you will feel better about yourself. This puts you in a very strategic position to receive many more blessings.

It was Zig Ziglar who reminded us that, "Gratitude is the healthiest of all human emotions. The more you express gratitude for what you have, the more likely you will have even more to express gratitude for." And I might add, "The more gratefulness we express, the more worthiness we have as human beings."

When you acknowledge things with an attitude of gratitude, your mood and perspective take on a whole new aura of positiveness. The gratefulness element keeps you keenly aware of the value of others in shaping your life. Regardless of how little you might think it is, being thankful for what you have opens the door for more meaningful conditions to prevail in your life. An "attitude of gratitude" will improve your altitude in sports—and in life.

"As we express our gratitude, we must never forget that the highest appreciation is not to utter words, but to live by them."
– John F. Kennedy

Consistency

This is one of the essential traits of an athlete. To reach an elite level, you have to execute your responsibilities and assign tasks with a high level of consistency. A necessary aspect of attaining this consistency is the ability to translate from practice to game situations with an elevated execution level. The expectation is always to strive to perform a little better each game.

Elite athletic status is neither magical nor mysterious. It is the natural consequence of consistently applying fundamentals. Whatever you want to achieve in sports will not come about without being consistent in the basics. Consistency sets the table.

It is important to recognize that to enjoy a higher echelon of success represents a feat just as substantial as what it took to get to that level in the first place. It takes a consistent and determined daily training effort to perform your very best every time you perform.

Consistency is behind the belief you will always come through… you will execute to the best of your ability…you will always strive to do the things you must do when you must do them. It is genuinely possessing the mindset that every opportunity counts for building a brighter future.

Consistency rises out of the feeling that you will give your best every time to receive the best. The height of your achievements will be solidified in direct proportion to the level of your consistency.

A SONNY MOMENT

Over my career, I have discovered that no matter where you are in your athletic development and what potential you have. No matter how much or how little you have gained. No matter how far you think you are from your sports goals–the power to move on, to improve, to master, to experience the exhilaration that comes from being an elite athlete is wrapped up in your personal traits.

Do you appreciate all the remarkable talent that you possess? Have you come alive to the seeds of the great potential within you?

That's right: within you right now is all the potential you need to become a better athlete. It may be immature and undeveloped–but it is there. And with proper mental and physical preparation and efficient application and usage, your potential will develop and grow.

So, nurture your potential. Stretch your limits. Work with the gifts that make you uniquely who you are. The fulfillment of your goal to be an elite athlete depends on releasing more and more of the undiscovered potential that can arise from quality personal traits. You unfold potential best when you see yourself as you can become–not just as you are.

Do you hear me saying to never put a limit on what you are capable of becoming? You take a big step in that direction when you develop the personal traits described in this chapter…and realize they can help turn your great potential into reality.

Do you want to know one reason why some potentially good athletes fail to make the grade? They are constantly comparing themselves to others. They keep their focus on what others have got or have done. They tend to believe others have more talent, get more breaks, enjoy more favours from coaches, or have a more satisfying athletic experience than they do. Envy and jealousy are their hallmarks.

This subject of envy has bothered me over the years. It has been my experience that there is a direct link between being envious of others and how athletes feel about themselves. The more envy they appeared to experience, the worse they felt about themselves. Maximizing your potential cannot occur when your focus is on others. Elite athletes don't waste time and energy concerning themselves with how others are doing. They don't lay awake at night thinking out loud about things like: "Is someone else getting ahead of me faster...getting more attention ...seemingly achieving more than I am."

Truthfully, can any of us live up to our potential when we are always concerned with what others have accomplished or the attention they are getting? Rest assured, the envy of others is a direct path to mediocrity. An envious nature will always be highly detrimental to the ability to perform at a peak level.

One of the hardest lessons for any of us to learn is to stand up and applaud the success of others–and mean it. There's room in the world of athletics—as well as life--for everyone reading this book to fulfill their potential and become the very best they possibly can be.

What others have done does not diminish the opportunity for you to do equally as well, does it? If anything, you should see if there's not something you can learn from those you may tend to envy by picking up a tip or two to improve your skills.

Do you have a standard by which you can gauge your best? Keep in mind that the key person in this determination is you. Your norm for doing your best has nothing to do with others. They may help establish the benchmarks, but doing your best according to your standards is the only standard that holds up daily.

We have realized the only valid comparison that counts for any athlete is the one made with the athlete you are today and the one you desire to be in the future. That is the only one that will have staying power over the long haul.

You don't have to blow out someone else's candle to let your own light shine.

PART

III

Preparing for Action

Chapter Eight

WHERE ARE YOU HEADED?

"A goal is a vision about where you would
like to be at some point in the future"
-Jim Rone

All action in sports occurs in terms of movement. The key factor behind all movement of any consequence is motivation. Motivation in the sports world can be described as a psychological driving force that arouses or reinforces action toward the desired goal of performing at peak capacity and creating opportunities for winning. Motivation evolves around both internal and external factors.

External motivation serves a role in moving athletes to action through the offering of awards and rewards. Unquestionably, winning the trophy can be a motivating goal. But over the long run, it is the internal factors of motivation that move the needle.

Internal motivation is a product of our purpose, values, and beliefs. It is the driving force behind seeing just how good we can be. Internal motivation is the only motivation that sustains through tough going and external stimuli that affects progress.

Strength to become the best arises from internal motivation where you do not feel the need to depend on outer incentives of any kind to get you going.

Internal motivation finds its place in those goals you set for yourself. Motivational goals are genuinely personal and rarely does performance rise above the level of where you set them. To soar high, sow big. And as Mark Twain once said, "If you aim high enough, you won't shoot yourself in the foot."

Internal motivation tends to work its way over and through goals that may appear uncomfortable to achieve initially. But once you get into working toward fulfilling those goals, they become even more significant motivators.

Critical factors in setting motivational goals includes questions such as: Does the sport you choose to play afford you the opportunity for the best distribution of your talents? Are you doing what you genuinely enjoy doing in an environment where you genuinely enjoy doing it? Your talents must be congruent with your sport. So, find a locker room that lines up with them and set your goals accordingly.

Sense of Purpose

As your purpose is, so is your will.
As your will is, so are your deeds.
As your deeds are, so are your rewards.

Do you have a crystal-clear purpose of what you want to accomplish in your sports experience? Your road to being an elite athlete begins with a solid purpose around which you build your motivational goals. This is the course you take in aspiring toward your athletic destiny. Real self-growth does not happen without purpose.

The backbone to becoming an elite athlete has at its base a purpose that arises deep from within your being. With a tremendous underlying purpose, you are prone to always to have direction. Your goals are more secure. Your focus is razor-sharp. Your potential is more pronounced. You tap into the reserves of energy, desire and courage easily and more readily with a strong sense of purpose. Purpose enables you to connect with your mission and be passionate about it.

How do you establish a greater sense of purpose in your athletic experience? It evolves from doing things that come naturally to you. Are you able to see opportunity amidst problems? Are you able to come up with solutions by thinking outside the box? Are you able to step out of your comfort zone and move beyond the status quo? Are you a natural born leader? Are you a gifted communicator?

Think of your purpose as being your mission statement. "I want to be…I want to do… I want to have…" The answers hold the purpose for your athletic experience. And the greatest purpose is doing something you can have fun doing.

With a true sense of purpose, you will tend to look at yourself--not as the athlete you are–but as the athlete, you can become. You will never grow beyond the athlete you are until you decide what kind of athlete you want to be.

Visualize Success

At its very beginning, purpose has a vision. From this visionary start, you formulate the purpose of what you would like to accomplish as an athlete. This vision enables you to develop into the kind of athlete you would like to be in the future. Maximize the use of your imagination. If you can imagine it, you can do it. If you can visualize it, you can become it.

Since your vision sets at the heart of your purpose, your vision becomes the centerpiece of establishing goals that take you further than the eye can see. Think about that. It would be best to never focus on goals considered easy to achieve. Let your imagination reach far beyond your horizon.

The imagination is the workshop where the construction of your future begins. It allows you to explore the possibilities and probabilities that can be created on the road to success. The imagination lays the pavement over which your reality ride eventually carries you.

On your visualized trips, imagine being and doing something special? Visualize your plan to proceed on the trip long before you begin the journey. Imagine the things that need to be done to reach the pinnacle of a triumphant destination. It is challenging to get from here to there, if you have no idea where 'there' is.

Follow your vision for it will accommodate the kind of environment where you grow and improve because you did something to help yourself grow and develop. It all begins with a vision…then you move on with action.

"The only thing worse than being blind is having sight and no vision."
-Helen Keller

"Goals provide direction. Where do you want to be after you have gone through a series of athletic experiences? A clear picture of where you are headed is crucial if these experiences are to lead to a successful conclusion."
-Jill Korrath

What you get by reaching a goal is not as important as what you become by reaching a goal.

"The road to success is built on a matter of choice... not a matter of chance. If you have no idea where you are going, how will you know when you arrive?"
-Mark Cuban

"Don't worry about trying to get ahead of others… the thrust behind your goals should be to stay ahead of your prior performance levels."
-Dr. Gaylon McCollough

Goal setting is like planning a trip: First, locate where you are. Second, decide where you want to be in a certain time period. Third, plan the route to get there.

"Goals just out of reach, not completely out of sight, are the best motivators."
-Robert Woodruff

"Individual goals are born in the heart and mind… and only there will they ever die."
-W. Clement Stone

Goal-Setting Keys

- Goal setting is done from the future back to the present. Learn from the past...plan for the future…but perform in the present.
- Set realistic, challenging, daily, weekly and seasonal goals that are desirable, believable and achievable.
- Set stretch goals, but don't set them so high they are rarely accomplished. Goals that just extend beyond the grasp have the best motivational value over the long run.
- To be effective, goals must be measured by quantity, quality, and time. Otherwise, they probably are not worth the time spent on identifying them.
- Write your goals down so you can see them...study them... refer back to them. This not only gives you a chance to check up occasionally to determine the extent of your progress, but it also creates focus, and what you focus on tends to expand.
- Goals to be reached must harmonize with action. In other words, goals are achieved on the back of daily action plans and execution.
- What obstacles, problems, and hurdles will stand in the way of achieving goals? Determine what must be overcome to reach goals. Then, plan to establish what needs to be done to push right through these roadblocks.
- Goals should be shared with those who can encourage and assist in achieving them. Getting them involved also reaffirms a personal commitment.
- Set a deadline for each goal. Some goals may have natural deadlines–the length of time, etc. But if they don't, set them. Without time deadlines, goals are limited in value.
- Always begin your goal-setting statements with the term, "I am…I will…I can…" Think in terms of what the action will look like as you work toward the end goal.

***If you go before you know where you want to go,
you are bound to end up somewhere you don't want to be.***

Creeds Need Deeds

What is the single action that, if taken, will enhance the likelihood of desired goals falling into place? Establishing a workflow pattern where your creeds mandate deeds is the answer.

The absence of a solid plan to be "deed conscious" leads to a tendency to focus on the most effortless tasks. There must be a consorted effort to extend your efforts so you can expand your base. Action must be broad enough and deep enough to perform deeds that reach goals and move forward.

The tougher the creeds, the greater is the requirement for appropriate deeds. Otherwise, you are just hoping for something good to happen. As Dr. John Maxwell states, "Hope is not an effective strategy in any undertaking."

A SONNY MOMENT

This goal issue is a big thing to me. I'm not sure that in this day-and-age young people are as goal-oriented as my era. Much of that is because there are many more variables to deal with today, making being definitive about where you want to go and what you want to do when you get there more difficult to pinpoint. Yet, I think it will serve any young athlete well to understand even the most generic notions of athletic success requires a path to run on and the willingness to navigate it. Define what it is that you want to accomplish on your athletic journey *before* you get too far into the trip is my suggestion

I think every young athlete needs to ask himself these questions: WHY do I want to be an elite athlete? "WHAT steps should I take to reach elite athlete status? WHERE do I draw the line on the type of goals I need to become an elite athlete? WHERE do I first begin the process of achieving goals? WHO do I need to help me achieve my goals? HOW is the best way to keep my goals front and center in my mind?

I have found that the elite athlete mindset has a strategic and formulated approach that evolves around specific goals. To say, "I want to be an elite athlete" is the ultimate goal. But this goal must take into account a lot of moving parts found in smaller, strategic goals. A wise move is to break down every aspect of what you need to do to align all the moving parts—so you can achieve your goals.

When there are clearly defined, specific goals, the principal thrust of your efforts will be in the direction of those goals. Because your goals are definitive, your entire goal strategy will ignite motivational alertness that will tend to carry you through thick and thin. The best predictor of your future is to establish a path of how to create it. Do it for you.

While it is essential to define your goals, you have to leave yourself some wiggle room for alterations. A critical factor in determining where you are headed is making quality adjustments on the journey. This creates a need for what I call re-directive thinking.

What we have found is the older we get, the less we like changes that challenge long-felt beliefs. Even an Act of Congress would not move many of us "old-timers" to make what could be beneficial adjustments in the way we do things. Too many of us prefer to live clutched to old trappings. We forego something better at the expense of continuing along the same old comfortable path, doing things the same old convenient way.

Fortunately, most of you reading this are young enough to welcome, even accept the need for adjustments in your travel plans. Let me offer a brief cautionary word: Stay away from the kind of thought pattern that takes goals as being static. When you reach a goal, it puts you in a position where you can see the next goal on the horizon.

The next chapter discusses the importance of learning and making adjustments. We are going to jump the gun and talk about what we call re-directive thinking. It applies to almost everything done.

There comes a time when to experience something different; there must be a genuine commitment to doing something different. The energy to pursue something different with vigor and excitement lies within the consciousness of envisioning how that "something" will ultimately enrich your athletic experience. It would be best if you were very deliberate at looking at your current level of play and determining what's not working as well as you like--or once was--and what redirection do you need to make.

Develop a comprehensive strategy that lays out clear goals and objectives for your athletic mission going forward. Suppose your present behavior or actions are not generating the kind of success you desire. In that case, the focus moves to re-directive thinking. You can concentrate on expanding your skills set and exploring ways to improve your overall performance levels and enhance your future growth. What I'm talking about here is the ability to be flexible and mobile in your thinking process.

The redirection questions before you are these: What are you willing to do differently? Are you willing to step out of your comfort zone and expand your play? Are you ready to explore new ways of performing and even venture into something that's unknown? Are you ready to reach beyond and grasp the future> something that has not been a part of your regular playing routine?

The type and size of the redirection you wish to make is based on your personal choices. Not your teammates. Not your coaches. What are you willing to do to prepare to be a better performer? The consequences of your choices will do one of two things: They either will help clarify your commitments toward what you have been doing, or they will lead you to make new decisions that will allow you to perform at a higher level more effectively.

Re-directive thinking demands action. The difference-maker is to make sure through your redirection, you are headed in the right direction. Redirection is a plus only if it is in the right direction. You may not always know for sure, but if you have done your homework, you know what direction in which you want to go—you know where you are headed. Now set your preparation course.

Re-directive thinking works best when there is a sustained effort to focus on improvement. The utmost learning laboratory takes place during those hours you spend training. Engaging in repetitive action during your training periods requires maximum attention. This will eventually bring to fruition views that arose during those moments you spent on re-directive thinking.

Chapter Nine

LEARNING BUILDS A FUTURE

The talent and ability to develop athletic skills are tremendous gifts. But athletic prowess must be secondary to educational growth and development. It is paramount that you embrace the attitude that education is your ultimate ticket to success in almost anything you do. It is the bridge over which will pass the very best things that you will get out of life. So, no matter your athletic dreams, obtaining a quality education is the soil in which those dreams do their best growing.

If you are a student, do you appreciate the fact that what you do today in the classroom will be a part of the rest of your life? This makes your wisest decision today, one where you apply yourself in the classroom with the same vigor and enthusiasm you have in the athletic arena or on the playing field. Work toward what you hope to become after your competitive athletic days are over. School-level sports careers do end, necessitating preparation for the next level.

If you keep doing what you have always done, you won't keep getting the results you have always gotten. That's because skills, methods, and tactics need to be constantly upgraded to keep up with the changes happening around you…and within you.

Nothing fails like success if it keeps you from learning new and better habits of performing … for to have it the way you want it, you must move beyond the way it is.

Learning is an Active Process

"You can't teach an old dog new tricks," is an old saying. The way we look at that statement may be true of dogs, but it is not true of human beings. As human beings, the ability to learn is not marked by years; it is marked by a state of mind. As another old saying goes, "Years will weather our hide, but to quit learning will weather our soul. Knowledge and skills know no age -- they never grow old."

How willing are you to set aside the old and reach out for something new? Some of the best things you learn will be learned after you believe you have learned everything you need to know. That may not be descriptive of where you are in your own personal development because of age, but the learning process is a forever thing.

The learning process can start anytime – anywhere… but you have to take the first step; you have to begin. You have to recognize the real significance of the act of learning is an active engagement. Once you have started, your mind will mobilize all its forces…your whole being will be involved in the effort. But you must take the first step; then you can grow from there.

The purpose of learning is always to keep intending to perform at a higher level. It will save you working to get better when you hold this attitude -- because a higher level is just one step or lesson away. It is important to remember that you only aspire to new heights when you are willing to say "Yes" to discovering and learning new and creative ways to perform. Always be a sponge. Learning is forever.

"The more you know, the more you realize there is to know. You need to know for sure that you are not ever going to know all you need to know about what you ought to know. So, keep on learning."

-Bob McCorkle

"Learning isn't expensive--ignorance is. So, don't be down on what you ought to be up on."

-Mark Twain

"Learning habits decide where you are going…but they also take you to where you have been. Learning new things involves unlearning old things."

-Dr. Ken Blanchard

"Good is the enemy of better and better is the enemy of best"…and "good enough is not good enough if better is possible." It appears that "the best way to make your good better is to work to make your better best." So, "stay with it until your good is better… and your better is best."

-Adapted from several sources

Experiencing Something Different

The root of all learning and the catalyst to begin the process of learning is simple. It starts by desiring the benefits of learning something new and different more than choosing the continuation of the status quo.

The adventurous nature of this consciousness is the desire to move headstrong into learning. The one thing that never changes is that everything is invariably evolving—there is always something to learn. Acceptance will keep you from doing the same old things in the same old ways and expecting different results.

Learning athletic skills entails a lot of realistic work. It requires extending in the direction of doing what you probably haven't done to add new dimensions of habitual growth to your sports activities. When you mentally move toward learning expansion, your capacity to change and adapt allows you to see possibilities you have never experienced before. This awareness will enable you to establish a foothold of what it will take to move you to the next level instead of continuing along a similar path.

The first phase of experiencing something different is a commitment to doing something different. We have said it several times, to have it the way you want it, you have to give up the way it is. The energy to pursue something that will add immeasurably to your future lies within the consciousness of envisioning how your capacity to learn is what allows you to move forward. One of the most consistent things you can count on is there will always be something new and different to learn and expand your horizon.

The next phase in the learning process is to follow actively and even seek out beneficial adjustments recommended by your superiors. If you don't change the right things, you can't expect to have upgraded your athletic experience, can you? Just make sure you are advancing in the right direction, for redirection is only a plus in the right direction.

Here are some other worthy thoughts on the learning process:

- Necessity has been called the mother of invention. Among us humans, it also can be called the mother of change.
- Be grateful for how something was beneficial to your past efforts. Be appreciative of what your past has brought you. But if now is the time to "let go," mentally prepare to move on.
- Not all performance modifications lead to growth, but there is no growth without alterations in the way you have been playing. Change is never fixed or static. It is an on-going event of awakening your internal ability to adjust and adapt.
- The motivation to move on beyond where you are can happen through the benefit of just a simple variation in your training regimen. This modification can get you moving in a more creative and productive direction.
- There is a world of difference between having a desire to improve and having an improvement plan. The more committed you plan to bring about improvement, the less complicated will be the improvement process.
- The longer you put off making upgrades to your skills and techniques, the longer it will take when you get to it.

- It is easier to discard personal responsibility for change than it is to accept it. Regardless of the change that is needed, most of us would say, "I'm doing okay with the way things are; why change now?" But familiarity is a battle cry that leads to mediocrity…or worse.
- The most oversized room for any young athlete is the room for improvement. Compete against yourself. Self-improvement is about being better today than you were yesterday.
- When you put a limit on how much you expect to improve, haven't you put a limit on how much you will improve.

Unless you are willing to leave some of your old points of view behind, you will seldom find yourself in a position to create something better--and possibly more lucrative-- in the days ahead.

Retrofitting

There is no place where you suddenly become great at anything that you do. Most overnight sensations take years to make a splash at what they do. They discovered that the route to top-notch performance is often slow and tedious.

This places the accent right on truly understanding why steady improvement is crucial if you are to enjoy future success. It means you have to undergo much trial and success. It means you must work hard to sharpen techniques, excellent skills, and improve attitudes, to reach an acceptable performance lev. It simply means you are always receptive to things that will enhance your play.

Have you given much thought to what holds athletes back and keeps them from seeking necessary improvements? Denial plays a prominent role. But it is okay to admit that you have limitations…you have made mistakes…you have experienced moments of weaknesses …you have found yourself powerless in the face of certain challenges.

The point is you cannot do anything about the future until you quit reflecting on the past.

Changing the course of what you want to accomplish in sports starts with a comprehensive strategy labeled *retrofitting*. Retrofitting is a term used to describe how you need to continuously make shifts in how you go about performing when your present behavior or actions are not generating the kind of success you desire.

The change in your current level of play does not have to be big. The type and size of change will do one of two things: They either will help clarify your commitments toward what you have been doing, or they will lead you to make more meaningful choices.

Quality athletic output depends on continual retrofitting. You cannot say there is nothing more to learn, no more skills to develop, no more challenges to be tackled, no more new tactics and techniques to try. It would help if you were never anxious about making appropriate changes in the way you perform, but that goes in the face of reality.

Enter a retrofitting mentality. It helps you adjust to the changes happening around you. It keeps you on your toes to actively seek out beneficial adjustments in your performance. Retrofitting sets at the core of your ability to move beyond the old ways of doing things when they can no longer guarantee high productivity.

Regardless of the sport, they each present a very persistent learning laboratory by repeating the same lessons until they are learned. So, analyze, evaluate and practice. That is what will bring you improvement to your game on an ongoing basis.

Retrofitting carries with it the responsibility of seeking new avenues for improving your performance base. A significant part of this responsibility is having a "now" attitude. Retrofitting doesn't start tomorrow or the next day, but now. It is on-going or non-going.

One final thought about retrofitting. It may very well mean that you have to delve into the unknown…into trying something new and different. You are probably not going to feel comfortable with it at first. But hang with it, you will soon get a handle on it.

Monotasking

What happens when you do not experience immediate success? Isn't there a tendency to forego the changes you have been working on after a few days, then gently slide right back into the old pattern?

Skills development occurs in stages. It takes time and effort to become an elite athlete. Focus on improving a single skill and direct your efforts toward improving that single skill. This is what has become known as monotasking.

Monotasking is the ability to embrace "one thing at once." The optimum for making positive changes comes through the ability to always focus on improving one skill–or even one step in executing that skill--at a time. Then, when you have mastered that step, it will spur you to master the next step. Then the next.

Now, don't expect to develop a skill overnight fully. Research shows it takes about three weeks of conscious effort and hard work doing what needs to be done for the change to take hold. Then you will need another month or so to get it firmly embedded in your mind and make it a significant part of your playing routine.

Practice Patience

Are you looking for someone to give you three easy steps to create mark improvement right away? Meaningful change takes time…and time takes patience. The power of patience is the result of invisible dividends. Time is working for you. Give yourself adequate time to reach your destiny.

When you have a solid plan for change that has been well thought out--one where you have considered all the variables--why shouldn't you give it a chance to work?

You have to consciously refrain from wanting to jump in and make frequent "adjustments." As you proceed with your three-week change pattern, wait as patiently and determined as humanly possible for it to work. After a while, your patience with pay off in a big way, as the upgrade you make becomes second nature.

Learn from Example

In sports, more is caught than is taught.

Example is one of the greatest teachers for learning skills and techniques...methods and tactics...that is, provided of course that you are receptive to new and better ways of doing things.

Are you thankful for the coaches and experienced players who show you how to perform the way you want to perform…who encourage you to improve and excel…who make you feel good about your ability? Attach yourself to a world of learning that benefits from the experience of others. These are some of the best resources available to you. Observe and listen to them with the intent of learning.

We believe all successful athletes share a common thread: they seek out the experience of a coach…a mentor…someone to rely on to help them. Neither one of us would be here talking about this without a coach who made a difference early in our athletic lives.

Who is the mentor in your life that provides you a chance to learn by example.? As a regular learning source, how attentive are you to absorbing the great information laid out for you? Learning is continuous for you don't know all you need to know about what you should know.

The talent and ability to develop athletic skills are tremendous gifts. But athletic prowess must be secondary to educational growth and development. It is paramount that you embrace the attitude that an education is your ultimate ticket to success in almost anything you do. It is the bridge over which will pass the very best things that you will get out of life.

Do you appreciate the fact that what you do today in the classroom will be a part of the rest of your life? This makes your wisest decision today one where you apply yourself in the classroom with an equivalent amount of potency and enthusiasm that you have in the athletic arena or on the playing field. Work toward what you hope to become after your competitive athletic days are over. School-level sports career do end, necessitating preparation for life away from sports.

As an elite athlete you may have an opportunity at the professional level in sports. But those jobs are few and far between. Just make sure you prepare yourself for a life away from sports.

If you keep doing what you have always done, you won't keep getting the results you have always gotten. That's because skills, methods, and tactics need to be constantly upgraded to keep up with the changes happening around you…and within you.

Nothing fails like success if it keeps you from learning new and better habits of performing … for to have it the way you want it, you must move beyond the way it is.

Scrutinize Carefully

Scrutinize what you hear from those who know little about you or what you do. Be careful of grabbing hold of someone else's opinion and making it your own because it sounds good. Carefully scrutinize, question, or test it before you accept it. "Will it work?" Brilliant revelations that bounce off the walls of your mind are only sufficient if they pass the application test.

What we are saying is to practice discernment. Be definitive about the kind of information you want to take to heart from others. Is it in line with the direction of your development? Define what will be helpful and what will not. Filter out what doesn't apply to you. Just be careful the information is coming from a trustworthy source. We are talking here primarily about people outside your inner circle.

The critical detail is to ask questions. There is no such thing as a dumb question, but you may get a dumb answer. Refrain from wanting to pretend you know something when you don't understand it. There is nothing wrong with saying, "I don't know." As someone so astutely said, "To say 'I don't know,' is a sign that you know what you know, and you also know what you don't know." Makes sense, doesn't it?

Gain Experience

We finish this chapter with some worthy thoughts about gaining experience:

- Experience helps us figure out just what isn't worth knowing.
- The best route to experience is being smarter today than you were yesterday.
- A smart, experienced player knows a lot, but doesn't say much about what he knows.
- Experience is not what happens to us...it's what we do with what happens to us.
- The experienced athlete knows the difference between pulling his weight and throwing it around.
- A smart athlete may know how to win an argument…but an experienced athlete knows how to avoid one.
- We all learn from experience...but some of us have to go to summer school to learn the lessons.
- Experience enables us to recognize a mistake the second time.
- Experience counts when we can take something from "this" to help us do better at "that."
- An education is what we get when we read the fine print ...experience is what we get when we don't.

A SONNY MOMENT

(for coaches)

A given in coaching is that there will be times when the playing season is not going well for a team. This raises two questions: How long does the coaching staff stay the course before they need to begin thinking in terms of retrofitting? Once that decision is made, what and how are the changes made?

I believe a coach can feel it in his gut when he needs to deal with the reality of making changes during the playing season. When things are not what they were expected to be; not even what they were hoped to be, there comes a time for a reality check. Sometimes the reason behind that reality check is not because a coach sees the light but because he feels the heat of the administration.

I can hear countless coaches saying, "This is who I am?" "This is what I believe in!" Okay. But be sure to ask yourself this one key question, "How is my way working for me now?" There is nothing that says alterations in the way you do things have to be significant. Quite possibly all you need is a series of small tweaks, here and there. I can assure you there comes a time, if you stay in the coaching business long enough, that you will need to grease the wheels to get moving again. I think I heard a few "Amens" from the back row.

It is human to be frustrated, discouraged, and dissatisfied when the wheels run off. Probably the first thing you need to do is to take the emotion out of the equation. That's not easy. It's downright painful when you struggle to move on beyond the tough sledding you have been experiencing. But it is imperative to start with a level head and work from an even keel to explore turnaround options.

The least appropriate way to approach change in my estimation, is through the old "if and but" technique. "If we had only done that," or "But we should have done this," has no place in making effective changes in the here and now. As the late Don Meredith would say on Monday Night Football, "If *if* and *buts* were candy and nuts, we would all have a Merry Christmas."

Be careful not to browbeat yourself over what has happened. There is always something more, and that something more has to be tackled with a forward-looking, solution-minded posture, not a backward-looking "if and but" approach. It's a time to consider all the angles, pull out all the stops, and hopefully, have something greater materialize.

The very motion of sports is toward seeking something more superior. A coach begins to seek what is better by first identifying those factors which have led to poor performance. Break these factors down into little pieces. Elsewhere in the book, we talk about monotasking—meaning to tackle one thing at a time. Be analytical. Why are you struggling? Where are things going wrong? What will it take to make it better? Toss around some ideas. Get ample input from the coaching staff. You probably don't need to reinvent the wheel; just fix a spoke or two. Set about eliminating the unproductive factors and begin cultivating those factors that can lead to future success.

There is one thing I think you need to be sure that you do, and that is to keep modifications as simple as you possibly can. You would be surprised how many coaches violate the simple principle and try to fit square pegs into round holes. There is a tendency to ignore the clear reality that cleverness in trying to devise craftier ways of doing things takes valuable time to implement and creates confusion. When you keep it simple, you learn quickly what your team can do. You also know very soon what they cannot do.

Once you and your fellow coaches settle on possible solutions, get everyone in the locker room on the same page. I tend to believe that words are the least reliable purveyor in sports. In every practice. In every scrimmage. In every game situation. The proof is in the demonstration—in the action. It is far better to actively show your players what changes and modifications are being made than talk about them. I'm not certain that you need to explain why you are making the changes. "This is us, in the future." The knowledge that can come from seeing it is more instructive.

***

"He's an in-game coach" is a term most pundits use in describing a coach who does a yeoman job of managing the game as it unfolds. The ability to make adjustments during the game is often the difference between winning and losing.

When everything else appears about equal, winning goes to the coaching staff who clearly sees what an opponent is doing and then readjusts their plan of attack accordingly. This "cat and mouse" affair can dramatically affect the outcome of a tense, competitive game.

There are also times when the game plan goes awry, and circumstances demand that the coaching staff resort to making adjustments because the team is not clicking on all cylinders. Adjustments during a game often are needed to give a team a chance to win. The secret is knowing when and how to make those changes.

Any alteration in the game plan does not necessarily have to revolve around obvious and recognized lines of attack--but it has to be done in ways that is best supported by your team's strength. Then it becomes a matter of steadiness and constancy in the players abilities to execute the adjustments in the game plan.

The need to bring about quality adjustments has its origin in one of these sources. It may come from:

- Perception of and careful observation of the inability of some players to execute the game plan.
- The noticeable and unexpected opponent's strength has created a need for change in the game plan.

Once a coaching staff gets a handle on the action going on, they can develop a different strategy to put the team back on track. It begins with an assessment of what needs to be done and how soon. To be effective, how the adjustment is explained to the players is very important. A coach must take care in presenting an orderly and tempered understanding of "What's next?" The coach's words and actions must outline how to produce better results…now.

My idea of making in-game strategic changes is probably somewhat different than most coaches. Sometimes you have to be what most would call impractical--some in the bleachers may even call it stupid. But it is often impractical thought from which excitement and fresh ideas arise to provide a more progressive route to a win.

The ultimate success of whatever changes the coaching staff proposes still lies with the players. For the adjustments made by the players to work, they have to be encouraged to focus on that which is present at the moment, giving little thought to the previous game action. Player's will best implement the in-game adjustments if the coaches refer to what happens next and spend no time harping on what has not been done up to this point in the game.

Chapter Ten

A WILL TO PREPARE

You must be willing to prepare at a level you have never prepared at before, if you expect to perform at a level you have never performed at before. In essence, to experience something different, you have to be willing to prepare to do something different.

Will to Prepare to Win

There is probably little difference between your athletic dreams and desires and those of almost any other athlete. All want to do well....to achieve something of significance...to be proud of themselves to have a significant degree of success.

To put the finger on the one thing that makes a difference in the level of achievement of most athletes, can be found in the will to prepare to win. The willingness to prepare is the little difference that makes the big difference in converting dreams and desires into reality. Without question, the road to success is built on the will to prepare to succeed.

Coach Paul (Bear) Bryant said, "The will to win matters… but in scheme of winning, the will to prepare to win matters much more." The most common cause of the lack of successful results is the absence of an aggressive will to win. But the will to win will be a frustrated desire unless there is an ever-present will to prepare to win. The base of this preparation is built on what a better future would like, feel like, be like. It is doing things you probably have never consistently done before.

Most athletes who have enjoyed tremendous success rarely were great in the beginning. But they were able to make themselves great because they knew they could be no better than the level of their preparation. They were aware they could only do what they were prepared to do. No more, no less.

"Prepare to do the things you are expected to do when you are expected to do them…so when it is time for the actual performance, you will do the things you are expected to in the way that you are expected to do them."

-Leonard Bernstein

"Highly successful athletes do not become successful doing things by the seat of their pants. They became successful through the long, lengthy hours of intense study, preparation and practice that helps make them successful."

-Bob Forsberg

To become an elite athlete, you have to understand why preparation is crucial. It means you have to undergo much trial-and-error. It means you must work hard to sharpen techniques, hone skills and improve methods and tactics, in order to reach a desirable performance level. It means you are always receptive to things that will help you perform better. Preparation connects you to a brighter future.

"The dictionary is the only place where achievement comes before preparation."

-Jim Boeheim

Developing Preparation Habits

Everyone wants to be a winner until they understand what it takes to be a winner. Unmet expectations become the norm if knowledge, learning and understanding lack the substance and direction that comes from developing quality preparation habits.

Until there is an acceptance that preparation habits are crucial to success, how successful can any individual player or team be? To sit back hoping that a little action here or there will be the magic pill that leads to winning results, is the epitome of disappointment. To change reality, the perception of preparation must change.

Successful game results are triggered by a rush of deliberate and continuous action in the preparation phase of any sport. Listen to these words of Coach Nick Saban: "Winning is a lot of hard work and preparation. You can't be complacent. Learn what you are supposed to do and be able to go out there and do it on a consistent basis is the backbone of winning."

Let us emphasize again, performing up to your very best level every time you compete, depends on your undertaking an intense and directed effort every time you train. Mechanics, techniques and the like depend on going full blast at every training session. That's the best way to learn your assignments and how to execute them inside and out, up and down, backwards and forward.

Thoughts on Preparation

- Preparation may not always bring success, but there is no success without preparation.
- It is not preparing for the things you like to do, that will make you more successful… It is preparing for the things you have to do to be successful.
- The fundamental theme behind all preparation should be to constantly move beyond what you are for the greater achievement of what you can become.

- A priceless performance at doing anything always will be preceded by paying the price at practice preparing for a priceless performance.
- Performing up to the very best level during every game opportunity is less a question of what you desire, as it is a question of what you are willing to do to prepare to perform at that level.
- The only way you can bring about improvement is to prepare in a way you have never prepared before.

"You will never perform any better than your
preparation habits allow you to perform."
-Paul (Bear) Bryant

Improving Preparation Habits

Two habits you must strive to eliminate...

- The habit of placing limits on yourself.
- The habit of letting others place limits on you.

The three stages of habits are:

- Stranger
- Companion
- Master (Good or Bad?)

A great way to improve your preparation habits is to:

- Seek the advice you need to have, not the advice you may like to hear.
- Be willing to attach yourself to those who know what you need to know.

A Matter of Habit

"My name is Habit. I am something that you created because of continual and similar behavior. I am your constant companion and closest friend.

Show me exactly how you want something done, and after a very short time, I will do it without your willful assent.

Most of the tasks you do will eventually become mine, because I am able to do them without question or hesitation.

I am one of your greatest assets, provided you have trained me properly. But if you have not prepared me properly, my actions will rob you of the opportunity to do something different and better. Rest assured this is the case."

-Author Unknown

"The big plays you make in a game are the little plays that you keep on making in practice better and better until they become a habit."

-Tom Izzo.

"Today, every practice activity...every game situation...every play connects you with the future. How you go about practicing today is going to be a part of the rest of your athletic career."

-Ralph (Shug) Jordan

"Perfect Practice Makes Perfect"

"Practice only makes a difference when you practice the right kind of practice. To put it another way: Practice does not make perfect...perfect practice makes perfect."

-Vince Lombardi

"Take pride today in your preparation for your practice habits make the difference in the improvement you muster."

-Tommy Tuberville

"A lot of players spend time talking about practicing better in the future never realizing a little of the future arrives every practice."

-John McKay

"The successful teams do not become successful on the day of a game, they become successful on the long, lengthy hours on the practice field."

-Gene Stallings

"If you are not making some mistakes in practice, you are not working at it hard enough."

--Duffy Daugherty

If practice doesn't challenge you, it won't change you.

"A great skill set is not something that's found...it is something that is created--one training session at a time."

-Bill Walsh

"More games are won or lost on the parched soil of the practice field than they are on the green grass of the playing field."

-Weeb Eubanks

"Great practice habits may not always bring success, but there is no success without great practice habits. The road to consistent winning run rights through the practice field."

-Vince Lombardi

Winners train, losers complain ...Don't whine, just grind.

Daily Mental Practice Schedule

- Yesterday's performance will not affect today's effort.
- I will make my biggest practice goal today one that out does yesterday.
- I will do something today at practice that will bring improved performance at what I am expected to do.
- I will do all expected of me today...and then some.
- I will perform today in such a way that tomorrow I will be better.
- I will not concern myself with tomorrow's schedule today until today becomes tomorrow.

"Practice works if everyone works at practice."
-Dale Earnhardt

A SONNY MOMENT

I want to share a couple of important topics with you in this segment: the way choices and consequences make a difference; and the role of preparation in your success.

Success in athletics–as in life--finds its footing in choices and consequences. The results of anything you do will be determined by the type of choices you make while performing. Some choices carry more weight than others, but no choice is inconsequential during game action. Every choice you make leads you inexorably to either success or failure in the execution of a particular play, or in a broader sense, the overall role you are expected to play on the team.

This is true whether you are practicing or in a game. Only you can choose how you are going to react to things happening around you and within you. This constitutes a great reason to understand why it is important to work at upgrading your choices so you can improve the consequences continually.

Buy into this choice/consequence concept and the role it plays in both sports and life. Embedded deeply in your psyche should be the reality that there is a consequence in every choice you make. Some of these choices are inherently more meaningful than others, In the bigger scheme of things, don't lose sight of the fact, consequence determine what happens, but it is the choice that sets the table.

I want to jump in and share with you the one thing that occurs in sports that doesn't necessarily apply to daily life; in sports, we know the results of the action right away. There is no tangible waiting period to see the consequences of any choices during a game or match. Doesn't that put the spotlight right on the essential nature of repetition?

The consequences will be instinctively different the more experience you acquire in making better and better choices. Repetition. Repetition. The right kind of repetition. It leads to more quality choices and more effective consequences

***

It has been my experience that the primary reason athletes with great ability fail to fulfill their promise is because of insufficient preparation. Part of the elite athletic mindset is to train every day. That doesn't always mean physical training. Elite athletes do have days of physical rest. But they use those days to review film, work on strategy, dissect their opponents, or simply have some "me" time.

The elite athletic mindset is about making small, incremental strides forward every day. There is no "just getting by" in the perspective of elite athletes. Elite athletes are constantly positioning and pushing themselves to do all they can to improve and get better…today.

Coaches can preach all day about the importance of a quality training effort. They can keep emphasizing to players why training is so crucial --why they should recognize and work at maximizing potential. But the answer is still in the individual player's work ethic.

Every player must take stock of the way training is approached by asking, "Am I putting out the effort to do what I'm supposed to do or what I'm capable of doing?" Athletes who focus on maximizing their capabilities, become better athletes. It is not any more elementary than that. And it is a beautiful thing to see.

Chapter Eleven

BRAINS IN YOUR MUSCLES

Those who are good are often separated from those who are great by their physical readiness to perform.

A guarantee in any competitive venue is there comes a time when physicality takes center stage. Elite athletes understand that must be physically and mentally ready to perform at all times. We believe the key to making that a reality is to develop "brains in your muscles."

If the laws of strenuous workouts, good diet and proper rest have been taken lightly, the body will be bankrupt of strength when strength is most needed. The result is when the body gives out, it takes one's positive attitude and desires to perform well with it.

> "Attitude plays a crucial role in overall health. It is the rule, not the exception in physical care. It is not a choice but a necessity to expand the practice of maintaining quality physical conditioning year-round. A positive, optimistic attitude about your body contributes royally to making it a healthy reality. Nothing will mean more to your success than being physically, mentally, and emotionally ready to perform to the best of your abilities–every time that you are in a competitive situation."
>
> -Dr. Bob Weil

"Take care of your body, you only get one."

-Yogi Berra

Pains = Gains

"Pain is temporary…quitting lasts forever."
Lance Armstrong

There are many certainties in sports. One that stands out to us is "you have to push your body and go through the pain to enjoy the gain." Sports are full of pain. Vigorous exercise, lifting weights, resistance training, and body trauma in contact sports, all produce various degrees of pain.

To build muscles, you have to encounter temporary, yet acute periods of pain that have been labeled as "microtraumas." The body responds to these "microtraumas" by building and bolstering the muscle tissue. Over the long run, these periods of pain lead to gains in strength, endurance, energy, and even self-confidence.

Elite athletes understand working out is not always fun, but they have come to realize there are immense benefits on the other side of pain. The more they push on through the pain, the stronger their bodies become to withstand the enormous physical requirements of sports participation. They keep leveling up, maximizing the gains. Elite athletes find solace in the varying levels of pain they experience because they realize the pain helps to prepare them to face any challenge.

To grow beyond your current physical development level, you must recognize the importance of the element of pain that comes from meaningful workouts. You cannot hide from pain, but you can grow from it. Your body thrives on the challenges offered by increased measures of pain. It's almost as if your body is saying, "Let me show you what I can do in the face of pain."

In the weight room or on the practice field, the pain you feel today is the strength you will need tomorrow. "No pain, no gain" is an old saying which is still highly appropriate. Or, like we prefer saying it: Growth in physicality means going through the pain to get to the gain.

Saying "No" to pain, makes it easier to saying "Yes" to gain.

Exercise Regularly…Forever

Your participation in sports provides you the chance to exercise regularly. What is worthy to note is the carryover value when you will not be participating in organized sports.

Both of the authors of this book are in the fourth quarter of life yet remain very active on the tennis court. Research shows that exercise can reduce the risk of heart disease, cancer, high blood pressure, diabetes, and other conditions. It also can delay the aging process.

We were deep in the writing of this book when I (Lou) contacted COVID-19. I spent 22 days in the hospital, including going through a very critical time early in my hospital stay. Eventually, I got better. What I want to share about this experience is the day I was released from the hospital, the doctor told me, "Mr. Vickery, those tanned legs helped to save your life." Being outdoors and exercising regularly was a critical factor in my being able to sustain life. Exercise, regularly.

One of the best benefits of maintaining a regular exercise program is that it positively affects maintaining a healthy body. Still, most notably, it produces a more beneficial cardiovascular system. This means the heart is better able to circulate blood to all parts of the body–even to our brains, improving memory and mental faculties as a whole.

Exercise can also improve appearance. It can keep us looking and feeling younger throughout our entire lives. Posture can be improved, and muscles become firmer and more toned. We not only feel better, but we also look better!

The pain you feel from working out today,
will be the strength you need tomorrow.

Warm-Up

Stretch. Stretch. Stretch those core muscles before engaging in physical activity. Improper warm-up is the basis for countless injuries which occur during play. We realize that most of you who participate on an organized team have well-heeled coaches in proper warm-up techniques. But even then, it is imperative to take the warm-up process very seriously. Think in terms of winning the warm-up.

While there is no one-size-fits-all warm-up procedure, there is no shortcut in preparing the body for physicality, regardless of the method used. Stretching and rotational movements that focus on specific areas of the body are a must during warm-ups. You can save a lot of potential pain and suffering by being proactive with the warm-up. The peril of a short warm-up is often found in a slow start once the game or match action begins.

Make sure every muscle in your body is primed and ready to go. The older you are, the more intense should be the *"getting ready for action"* part. We are great believers in using exercise bands or stretch ropes to activate the larger muscle groups. Five good minutes of stretching and pulling can lead to a highly effective start when the action begins. But it requires time, discipline, and effort to make it worthwhile.

"Pause for the Cause"

Learn to unwind so you will have something in the tank when it is time to wind back up again.

One of the more difficult things for active people to do is to take a "pause for the cause." There are times when you need to slow down and back off a bit and relax when you are not actively engaged in the athletic environment.

Taking a self-restoring timeout is as much about a mental gain as it is a physical gain. This "timeout" gives the creative juices a chance to flourish. It gives you a chance to think through ideas and solutions buried under the hustle and bustle of daily activities.

A wise move is to establish a goal-free zone where you have nothing planned...where there are no deadlines, responsibilities, or places to be. Such a zone allows you to unwind, regroup and just be yourself. This is a great tool to get a new perspective on you…and a clearer picture of academic and athletic life.

"Fatigue makes cowards of us all."
-Vince Lombardi

Healthy Habits

Always be on the lookout for ways and means to help develop more health-conscious habits, including:

- An environment away from the playing field or arena free of things that could lead to unhealthy addictions.
- A lifestyle that encompasses good nutrition, plentiful sleep, and ample life-defining moments with family and friends.
- Mental and emotional balance that allows for optimism, happiness, and satisfaction.
- Conditions that are free of oppressive and divisive factors like fear, anxiety, and depression.

"What You Eat--You Are"

In the age of fast food, it is often difficult to eat the right food and in the right amount. Willpower tends to take a back seat when you are hungry, and there is a fast-food restaurant near at hand. There is often a struggle between will and temptation. When temptation takes over, we generally end up eating more of the wrong kinds of food.

Eating right is super essential to becoming an elite athlete. It is crucial to be actively conscious of the food you eat. It is no easy task to change eating habits, but it has a real ring of importance if it is needed.

Like correcting any long-term habit, it takes mental toughness to change eating patterns. A smart move is to establish a strategy for eliminating lousy eating habits. Try the following on for size:

- STOP TO EAT. When it is time to eat, just eat. Drop what you are doing and focus on eating. You will enjoy it more and find that you won't need to eat as much food, either.

- SIT TO EAT. Eating on the run causes us to grab a snack later on. On the go, we are less aware of the amount of food we have consumed. Sit down at a table to eat, even if your food arrives in a bag.

- DON'T SHOVEL. Slow down and enjoy your food. You will experience less bloating as well. Swallowing air leads to bloating and can create gas. The same occurs when you talk with your mouth full. Take in smaller bites, eat slowly and chew your food with your mouth closed.

- STOP EATING BEFORE YOU ARE FULL. Put your fork down at the first tinge of fullness. This gives your brain a chance to realize you are full before you overdo it.

- REDUCE YOUR SNACKS. Do you tend to over-indulge in calorie-laced products between meals? The best rule is to cut back on snacking. It keeps the stomach "turned on," leading to the habit of overeating.

- WATCH WHAT YOU SNACK ON. Okay. If you are a "snacker," let your choice of a snack fall within the 10/5/20 rule. This rule establishes snacks should have no more than 10% fat, 5% carbohydrates, and 20% sugar of the daily requirements. Even then, eating snacks always evolve around moderation.

- EAT WITH OTHERS. Research shows eating with others tends to restrain eating behavior. By taking time to talk and share, you eat more slowly, which registers more quickly on the brain that you are full.

Protein

Protein is the primary source from which the body derives energy. Sports require a steady flow of energy to keep up with the demands of the activity level. This places the accent on ensuring you eat enough protein to keep up with your daily needs.

The protein you eat is broken down into amino acids that are needed for optimal health and athletic performance. The body cannot produce all the amino acids required, necessitating eating foods with protein.

Enter meats. That is the source for most protein intake. But how much protein is required for a growing and developing athlete? Let's make it simple: Take your weight and multiply it by 0.75 grams of protein per day. Now take that number and divide it by the number of meals you consume a day. For example, if you weigh 180 pounds, multiply this number by 0.75 and come up with 135 grams of protein per day. Then divide this number by the number of meals/snacks (4) you do a day, and you find you need to eat 33.75 grams per meal/snack.

It is imperative you not gloss over the amount of protein you are eating daily. Your energy level and ability to maintain a consistent performance are dramatically affected by your protein intake. Not getting enough protein may negatively impact not only your performance level but your growth and physical development, as well.

> "More and more research points to the lack of proper nutrition as the cause of many of our health issues. The food you eat and the way you eat will make a significant difference in your energy level and the quality of your performance. It is crucial to your overall health that you be tough with yourself at the food line. Listen to your body. It tells the whole story."
>
> -D.P. Vickery

> "A great way not to overeat is to focus on 'crunch time'. That is the sound we hear as we chew food. It has a ring of 'crunch', doesn't it? The expert opinion is to 'chew like a cow', which is slow and methodical. The "crunch" sound is a cue--if we listen to it--that tends to make us more aware of regulating how much food we intake."
>
> -Dr. Ted Broer

Hydration

Drink plenty of liquids. Drink even more liquids than that, if you are to remain hydrated during physical activity. In fact, hydration is essential to peak athletic performance. More importantly, it is essential to health safety. When you do not consume enough water or eat plenty fresh fruits and vegetables to stay properly hydrated, you can create all kinds of health concerns for yourself. Hydration is one those often-overlooked conditions that needs to be brought front and center.

Drinking enough water each day and staying hydrated is crucial for the following health reasons:

regulates body temperature
helps the heart more easily pump blood
keeps other organs functioning properly
maintains body muscle tone
assists the brain to work efficiently.
aids in digestion
keeps joints lubricated
prevents infections
helps the heart more easily pump blood
keeps organs functioning properly
delivers nutrients to cells
fights fatigue
prolongs endurance
improves sleep quality

For you younger athletes, all those sweetened and sugar-laced beverages that many of you consume are not the answer to staying hydrated. Energy drinks, sodas, vitamin waters, even too much fruit juice, according to the experts, do more harm than good in the hydration factor. We probably stepped on a few toes with that bit of information.

Another word of caution; while not common, it is possible to drink too much water. When a large amount of water is consumed in a short period of time, it can dilute the sodium levels. Feelings of light-headedness and dizziness are symptoms of too much water--too fast. This can also put additional strain on the kidneys as they attempt to rid the body of the liquid overload.

How much liquid each day? Depends of the type of activity, but on the average experts recommend drinking roughly 80 to 108 ounces a day. That's a lot of trips to the rest room for some of us.

A SONNY MOMENT

Over the years, I have had many players with great physical tools and upside potential who had to be really pushed to blossom. I genuinely believe an essential role for coaches is to challenge players on who and where they are in their physical development and their capabilities in developing physicality in the future.

A lot of promise is just that for unpolished players with loads of potential who need to get stronger, stricter, and more durable. This transformation in my book begins in the workout room. Physicality in sports is initiated from the ground up. Without strength in the feet, ankles, and legs, any athlete will be hard-pressed to play effectively.

Think about it: The ability to move quickly and efficiently is dependent on what happens at your base. Your base is imperative to developing the solid reactionary forces needed in sports acceleration and mobility. Then from this ground floor beginning, you can extend the muscular structure and grit of the rest of the body.

When you work out on a routine basis, your muscles build up greater endurance to perform physical movement and activity. I have had a few players who were workout freaks. They would attack the most mundane and painful workouts as if they were a privilege.

It has been my experience that healthy-minded athletes are the ones who take care to be moderate in their indulgence. Follow me closely on this one: how you treat your body should be patterned on the rules of good health and well-being, not on pleasure. The excellence and dignity of taking care of yourself doesn't mean you abandon luxury and pleasurable living; do it in moderation.

Grasp that physical fitness is the route to a brighter future. Gain a more incredible knowledge of how to develop your talents and abilities. Become a strict discipline of working out and building on your strengths. Win the physicality battle to help become an elite athlete.

Chapter Twelve

TIGHT-KNIT LOCKER ROOM

It is our firm belief there is one thing that can further the mental readiness of a team (this includes everyone associated with a team) before the first game or match is ever played. That's the team leadership setting the stage for creating a tight-knit locker room. Leaders take a big step in this direction when they establish core team values to help guide everyone associated with the team during any team and game activity. These values are not just words on a piece of paper but are well-thought-out and packed with meaning, significance, and direction.

We can hear a couple of questions being raised from the back of the room: What are core team values? Why should a team have them?

First, values are preferences based on what is determined as the most desirable response in any situation. Every day in sports--and in life--athletes encounter problems that challenge them to decide what is right or wrong, good or bad, just or unjust, and even why they play sports. Some of these situations are unique, many are routine, others are of extreme importance. Behind almost everything an athlete does—every choice made, every action taken—is a system of values. These values vary from individual to individual, but they will play a vital role in any team activities.

The answer to the second question is grounded in the fact the core values are the principles established to guide actions and conduct from administrators to coaches to the water boy, even to parents and fans. These core values serve to define proper behavior for those who are associated with the team. While they may not outline potential consequences for improper behavior, they form the basis for rules and regulations covering unsuitable conduct.

The team core values provide a keen sense of direction and focus for all team members. There is no guessing about what is expected when core values for those associated with the team have been clearly defined, as well as implicitly and explicitly presented to all.

Thinking and doing the right thing and valuing the established rules and regulations reflect a true spirit of professionalism, and form the foundation of a team's culture. By creating intentional and proactive core values, a team develops an ingrained culture that is grounded in the team's DNA. This serves as the driving force in helping a team to rely on each other as it strives to reach its full potential. A team with a quality culture is more readily able to adapt and adjust to conditions that don't go exactly how they were expected to go.

Now for the critical step: identifying applicable team core values that best fit the character and make-up of the team. Team values that are chosen wisely and discriminately by coaches and leaders provide direction, discipline, fun, and purpose in all the activities a team engages in on a regular basis.

Ten team values that we want to share with you in this chapter, include the following:

1. Sportsmanship
2. Respect
3. Teamwork
4. Interactional Skills
5. Diversity Sensitivity
6. Enthusiasm
7. Skillfulness
8. Work Ethic
9. Competitiveness
10. Have Fun

There are a ton of others to choose from. One not on the list is leadership. Sonny will address that in his SONNY MOMENT. We will have added comments about some of the values disbursed throughout the various forthcoming chapters in the book. The key is to read these with an eye toward how they might apply to you.

Personal Core Values

The key to creating and sustaining the team's culture is dependent on the workable core values of each individual who is a part of the team. These core values are best measured by how they connect with team values that have been posted. The more closely aligned personal values are with team values, the easier it is for any athlete to function within the confines of the team's culture.

Personal core values provide meaning and direction for team members. But these core values go well beyond the playing field to reflect the behavioral and social aspects exercised in daily life. The longer athletes play sports the greater will be the respect for, and application of, core values in all that they do.

It is important to note team core values extend far beyond the players on the team. There are significant situations and critical moments when the actions, conduct, and behavior of all administrators, coaches, management, and staff reflect the team's core values. Strictly from a player's standpoint, a player must apply these core values in playing situations, meeting fans, talking to media, on the practice field, in the dressing room, and when interacting with coaches and teammates. The key here, in our estimation, is to make core values count for something exceptional. Unless they are credible and concise, they are not worth the time and effort spent putting them together or even talking about them.

Sportsmanship

Pay attention to your thoughts. for they become beliefs...
Pay attention to your beliefs, for they become values…
Pay attention to your values, for they become attitudes…
Pay attention to your attitudes, for they become actions …
Pay attention to your actions, for they become habits…
Pay attention to your habits, for they define character…
Pay attention to your character, for it forms your destiny.

-Adapted from an unknown source

Character and reputation are at the center of any display of sportsmanship. Character is what you are—your private substance. Reputation is what others think you are—your public image.

A reputation is a message about you that grows and travels by word of mouth. A reputation, however, is a fragile thing. Should you compromise on character, it can be easily fractured.

Upright character is the only sound foundation for a solid reputation. The character of your play is based on your overall character. It has been our experience over the years that "Competition not only builds character, it reveals character."

In Chapter Seven, we talked about how integrity sets right at the heart of the development of sportsmanship. Integrity is the major ingredient of character. It is a constant in building honesty and truthfulness. Integrity resides at the very core of one's reputation, laying the foundation for sportsmanship.

In any form of athletics, sportsmanship has no peer. It is the lasting power of your desire to do the right thing. Be mindful of a clear picture of the kind of sportsmanship you want to display as a player. Then, act accordingly to that image. Don't ever forget whatever choices you make serve to make you who you become.

Always be a beacon of sportsmanship. Answer with an unqualified "Yes," the challenge of doing what is right because it is right. It is not always going to be easy because many times you are moving against the current. But that's the right direction. So, establish your course. Plant your feet. Build a foundation. Then, there will be no questions about how you will play.

There is one other issue about good sportsmanship we want to discuss. Sportsmanship doesn't come automatically or effortlessly to every young athlete. This is especially true after a tough loss. This is when the emotions can overrule logic. A problem? Work at it diligently.

We believe athletes must do three things after every game. First, seek out members of the opposing team. Shake hands or trade high-fives or exchange fists bumps, and tell the opposing team "good game." This shows the opposing players that you respect and appreciate them.

Second, if your team has won the game, celebrate your victory, but don't stand around bragging, boasting or making fun of the losing team. Nothing is earned by putting an opposing team down. It's okay to enjoy a win, but show respect for your opponent while doing it.

Third, be courteous when you lose. You know you are not always going to end up on the winning side of the ledger. Take responsibility for your losses instead of bad-mouthing the other team, or blaming the loss on something or someone else, notably the officials. Use these three tactics to upgrade your sportsmanship.

A young player who is taught about sportsmanship learns a great deal that will be valuable in life: how the rules are made to be followed; how to play fair and square; how to be humble in victory; how to lose without becoming emotionally upset; and also, how to give a victorious opponent full credit. All these prepare for living with integrity.

Respect

Respect is an essential component of both personal identity and interpersonal relationships. Respect can best be defined as esteem, honor and a sense of the worth of someone or something.

Respect is the epitome of the way you treat others around you. It is what you want in return. As it relates to team members and coaches, respect is a crucial aspect to the functionality of a team being united as one. To be a team—everyone has to be united as one. The epitome of respect is when all work together for the good of all.

We hope you get the picture that respect for others is fundamental. However, understand you will value others only to the extent of the respect you have for yourself. As you increase the respect for your self-worth, you enhance your ability to receive value in return. Your self-respect increases your potential value to the world around you. Wrap your hands around that truth!

You must understand that self-connection creates the confidence needed to bring a higher value to your external connections. You enter the process of interacting with others on the team at a higher plane when you feel truly confident in who you are. When you positively honor yourself, the true value will show in the way you approach coaches and teammates and how they approach you. There's no question, the more you produce something greater in the way you feel about yourself, the better will be the respect others have for you.

Our intention for much of the material in this book is to elevate your self-respect. As your respect for yourself grows, so does your ability to value and honor the words and actions of your coaches and teammates. You will find yourself increasing the depths of your connections because you are coming across as trustworthy.

One final thought on respect before we move on. Possess the utmost respect for an opponent. The loss (or minus) column is full of those who underestimated an opponent. Respect is an impeccable part of preparation leading up to a game and during the game. Just think, if you had no opposition, there would be no reason to play the game in the first place, would there?

Teamwork

Teamwork works—when everyone works.

You do not lose yourself in sports by being a great teammate—you find your best self. You will never know how much you are truly worth to yourself until you know how much you are truly worth to the team. Progress in any team sport depends on the understanding that if you want to help yourself, you can only do so by giving your all to the team effort. Below are other thoughts on teamwork:

- There is no "I" in team.
- The term "team" has no meaning except the meaning given to each team member.
- WE always outplays ME.
- A real team has more 'we go' and less 'ego.'
- A team's strength is built around unity and a feeling of oneness.
- The more a team accomplishes, the less anyone should be concerned with who gets the credit.

- The main ingredient in being a star is the support given by the rest of the team.
- "The most valuable player on the team is the one who makes the most players valuable." -Peyton Manning
- A real team effort depends on everyone on the team pushing up, not pulling down. The strength which team member gives to each other will be there when it is needed.
- The team members who prefer to do it alone do not win nearly as much as the team with the best TEAM players.
- "Teamwork-works," when each member of the team works.
- Just remember: "None of us will ever be as good as all of us."

-Selected from various sources

"Applaud your teammates efforts, acknowledge their successes, and encourage them to do their very best. Everybody wins when teammates help one another."

-Bill Parcells

Your emphasis as a teammate should be on being a great teammate. Regardless of how insignificant you may think your role is in the larger scheme of things—being a top-notch teammate serves you personally in two ways: It helps you counteract any self-defeating thoughts through your association with positively supportive people; and their encouraging words help you to confidently move forward in your quest to advance your athletic skills.

Enthusiasm

Be the captain on your team in charge of enthusiasm.

To be successful in sports calls for a high-intensity level and full-fledged flow of adrenaline. While involvement is essential, it means little without playing with enthusiasm.

Enthusiasm arises from an excitement and strong interest in what you are doing. It is an incredibly powerful tool in generating the adrenaline needed sustain action. Enthusiasm can create an overall feeling of well-being with many worthwhile side-affects such as energy, willpower, and fearlessness.

You can rarely play in an extraordinary way without enthusiasm being in your playbook. Enthusiasm is one of those things that gives you a chance to have a sustaining relationship with success. As long as it is a part of your activity level, your effort will remain high.

Just for the record, happiness has its base in enthusiasm. Being happy about what you do emanates from being enthused about doing it. Think about that for a moment.

Enthusiasm is like any other worthwhile attribute, is the result of conscious effort. Because it rarely comes naturally, enthusiasm first must be generated internally. Then it has to be continually practiced and exercised to remain a part of who you are.

It is important to understand that while enthusiasm is an individual thing, it is never purely a personal matter, for it not only affects your efforts but it also has a big positive effect on others.

"ENTHUSIASM defies the laws of mathematics,
for when you divide it, it multiplies."
-Tom Peters

Without Enthusiasm…

All that you know is incomplete.

All that you think is insufficient.

All that you believe is insignificant.

All that you do is inadequate.

Enthusiasm is the difference in making any event a great experience.

Interactional Skills

We see interactional skills, or lack thereof, as one of the biggest challenges facing the development of team togetherness. The inherent ability to effectively communicate and interact with others is an important value in a locker room. It is however often an illusion and somewhat vague trait. We have found it is a vital function of collaborative behavior between all those involved with a team. All team members need to understand and appreciate that an effective pattern of relational and interactional skills leads to successful communication among team members.

Interactional skills are established and time-honored when you undertake the process of creating a reciprocal mutuality with those who are around you regularly. This mutuality is accompanied by words, listening, actions, and unspoken expressions of care and concern. Being interactively savvy is essential when establishing positive relations with those that you share a common team purpose. This first-hand reality requires the transparent exchange of information, sharing ideas, and the opportunities for building solid connections and relationships.

Much of the interaction between people today is transmitted with two fingers on an electronic device for better or worse. There are many benefits to the social media way of communicating and interacting that permeates today's society. There also are significant pitfalls detrimental to building a solid relational base that is so important to team interaction. On behalf of all, collective interactional efforts add a measurable sense of permanency to what goes on in a locker room.

Reflect a moment on what is going on in your locker room. How deeply rooted is the breadth and depth of the relationships you have with teammates? What are you doing to develop and build more profound and visibly meaningful personal relationships?

Innate to the human character is the quest to be social. Human nature craves human interaction, and interaction cannot be effectively replaced by technology. While technology will continue to grow as time moves forward, the value of personal friendships and relationships will play a key role in ensuring a team's success in the future. Our take is that quality relationships between yourself, other team members and coaches, are essential.

Set yourself a goal of consistently communicating and interacting with as many of your teammates as you possibly can regularly. A great way to do this is to improve the quality of your listening. This will in turn improve your ability to connect with and interact with others.

Our Maker was telling us something when He gave us two ears and only one mouth! There is little doubt developing communication skills starts with your ears, not your mouth. To get to know people better, listen to them better. You can learn a lot about an individual simply by listening with the purpose of gaining a better understanding, not only of the conversation but also of the person. As Yogi Berra so astutely said, "You can see a lot by listening."

Team relationships are created, nurtured and developed with expectations they will grow and improve the "togetherness" that is vital to a team's success. These relationships cannot be manufactured, designed or forced. They are established when you create the right kind of interactional skills and a climate to grow and cultivate them.

Diversity Sensitivity

We can tell you in this day and age, diversity is an essential concern on a team. We thought about putting the diversity issue under the previous heading on interactional skills, but it is too important not to assign it a separate title.

Diversity to us extends far beyond race or ethnic group. It encompasses age, personality, background, speech style, and more. Most sports teams are made up of players from different cultural backgrounds. Showing sensitivity, treating others as equals, being flexible, and striving to find creative ways to work through cultural barriers have as much to do with team unity as does anything. It is encumbered upon each team member to make this a priority.

Developing respect for a diverse group of people is a highly valued quality in building team chemistry. There should be the right to be different and to be respected for that difference. Differences that are not too extreme can be positive because they create a unique identity. This means that since individual differences exist, it is vital for every team member to understand all associated with a team are due respect for the simple fact of who they are.

Do you hear us saying that you owe your teammates a basic level of respect, even if you do not approve or share everything they do? Respecting others is not judging them by their attitudes, behavior or thoughts. It is accepting them as individuals and all the power the word "individual" carries with it.

The challenges that are ever-present on a diverse team bring to the forefront authenticity and the influence of esteem. Marching orders are simple: continue to upgrade all aspects of the challenges embedded in diversity. Work to grow more powerfully and convincingly your respect for everyone associated with the team. That outlook will serve you well anywhere and at any time with people from all walks of life.

Skillfulness

We think the message to be conveyed here is reasonably evident: Constant enhancement and improvement in your foundational skills base should be your standard of performance. The process of skills growth is tied to the desire to want to learn.

Learning is a process. Skillfulness is a result of the process. Skills development is established through learning upgrades that lead to more sustainable skills expansion. The more you learn about doing something, the fewer surprises and obscurities you encounter in the future. Over time, everything becomes either more apparent or suggestive of something else. This in turn leads to another possible learning experience… and then another. That is skills progression.

Growth in skills is never static. It is stimulated by instructive and inspiring behavior, where you continually seek ways to enlarge your skills base and expand your ability to perform. The challenge is learning how to become highly proficient in the practice time allotted and do it with the highest degree of dependability. Instinctively, seek to learn the correct action in the right way. Be as realistic as possible in emulating actual playing circumstances. This is the basis for developing, expanding, and building a solid base of skillfulness.

Our experience is that the learning process is best served by being attuned to the originality of daily improvement. Concentrate on making incremental progress daily. This thought progression leaves the obscurities of the future and the boredom of the past at the door. The now moment is always the best learning moment.

When seeking ways and means of expanding your skills base, understand progress can move rather slowly. It would help if you appreciated that you cannot conquer everything at once. Discovering and growing new and different skills takes time.

The challenge for many young athletes is that if they don't receive instant success or gratification, they get discouraged. They want what they want now, and if they don't get it now, they walk away and quit. That hasn't been your history, has it?

The one big difference between those who demonstrate the desire to stay the course, and those who give up and go on to something else, is patience. The lack of patience is one of the major reasons why many athletes fail to enjoy solid skills enhancement.

Too many athletes are looking for coaches to give them three easy steps on how to be successful at what they do–and they want these steps to create and engender enormously immediate progress. But meaningful skills growth takes time…and time takes patience.

When you have fully implemented skills growth in step with your athletic purpose, you need to give those actions time to materialize. You didn't get to the point of needing corrective action yesterday, and effective change will not be visible overnight. Patience. Practice patience constantly. You must give any newly acquired skills a substitutive chance to make a difference in your performance.

Work Ethic

Work ethic arises from both physical capacity

and a steadfast and determined will to win.

Why is it an athlete with only average ability consistently performs above average, while another athlete with exceptional ability regularly falls short on quality results?

A significant part of the answer to this question can found in an athlete's work ethic. Work ethic is a core value based on durable work and diligence. Those athletes with strong, positive work habits tend to demonstrate that they can get a leg up on the competition by working harder and wiser.

Work ethic is an inherent attitude that athletes develop about themselves and the quality and depth of their work efforts. Those athletes with inadequate work ethics tend to do just enough to get by and eventually develop a reputation for lazy work habits. After hearing about it from coaches and teammates for a length of time, their lack of quality application can eventually become a part of their belief system. That's a reputation that takes a whole new philosophy to overcome.

What is your philosophy of work ethic? Do you possess a high level of intensity in your work patterns? Spending time focusing and developing the best work habits you possibly can muster leads to more positive outcomes.

Those athletes with solid work ethic are intrinsically motivated to do their best and are rewarded by delivering consistently high results. Through sheer willpower and determination, they place a high value on doing what is expected of them to the best of their ability.

Elite athletes realize performing well can never be regarded as incidental or accidental. It is a direct reflection of their attitude toward their responsibilities to themselves and their teammates. Drawing on their strong work ethic helps them to continually develop their skills.

The experience of working harder and getting more done in less time creates more growth opportunities. Buried deep in applying yourself with a strong work ethic is how it speeds up getting to the "good part" faster. Applying yourself in a bigger and broader way will lead to getting more done. That's a worthy goal.

Hard work beats ability when ability doesn't work hard.

Competitiveness

Both of us have seen numerous athletes over the years who had a chance to be great but lacked the competitiveness necessary to put them over the top. The ability to be competitive is a team core value that cannot be any more personal. Believe us, the higher you expect to go in any sport, the more competitive you must become. The reason is simple enough: the higher up the success ladder you hope to climb, the more formidable the competition you will face.

Possessing a strong desire to be the best at the role chosen for you to play is the centerpiece of competitiveness. But you must apply common sense and not let your competitiveness override your better judgment in your drive to be the best. Just possess balance in your endeavor to be more successful as a competitor.

Digest these great words on the reality of the competition:

- The size of the competition is about the same size as your overall attitude toward the competition. The right attitude is that the competition is competing against you…not you against the competition.
- If you become afraid that the competition is better than you are, at some point the competition will be.
- The key to enhancing your competitiveness is to focus on what you can do, not on what the competition may or may not be able to do.
- It is hard to sometimes to live with tough competition, but it is harder to live without them. They motivate you to work harder—and smarter.
- Never underestimate the capabilities of any competitor. The lost column is full of those teams who have taken their competitors lightly.
- Good competitors provide a clearer picture of what you have to do to become better. They give you a real sense of your level of competitiveness, and will show you what you must do to improve.

- Overcoming the challenges of the competition is the only way to develop and build a future—quality competitors produce the soil in which you will do your best growing.
- If it were not for the stiff competition that you face, what would you do with yourself? Be thankful for the strong competition you encounter. It gives you a chance to see just how good you can be.
- A competitive situation is a natural habitat for a winner. Winners study their competitors' strengths and weaknesses ...their tendencies and tactics…their game plans. Winners simply know their competition.

Let the game come to you. Without something challenging you, there is no possibility to improve your performance.

> "Your teammates ordinarily test you at practice, but the real test is provided by your game day or match opponents. So, from this standpoint, you can consider your opponents to be great teachers, and you need to be thankful they give you the chance to learn how to get better."
>
> -John McEnroe

Have Fun

Surprised? That's right. No fancy title here: Simply have fun. If you cannot have fun doing something, why do it?

Sports participation can be very intense and demanding, lessening the joy you can receive from being involved with it. Unless you find something within the sports experience to revitalize your spirit and make you feel great on the inside for doing it, you will be hard-pressed to play at an elite level.

There is no doubt that the ability to sustain motivation comes from loving what you do and the enjoyment you receive from being a team member and interacting with others. The drive required to perform any task effectively is more readily accessible through the power generated from the energy of interacting with teammates. The instances of experiencing celebratory occasions and successes enhance the delight and pleasure that comes from team participation.

The fact of the matter is that having fun plays a vital role in being successful in any sports activity. Below are some essential benefits of the role fun plays in sports participation:

- Provides perspective
- Enhances the ability to adapt
- Increases retention
- Enhances interest
- Improves spontaneity
- Increases productivity
- Defuses stress

A SONNY MOMENT

How important is it to have a team culture built around impeccable team values? Ask this question of any Hall of Fame coach, and the answer you get will probably differ for each one. To answer this question, here's what I see as crucial to developing team unity.

I think a coach's biggest task and his greatest joy is to see his players mature and grow as human beings, and become productive members of society. A coach lives consciously for himself, but unconsciously he serves as an instrument for the achievement of those around him. I don't know who said it, but this quote fits right in with what I am talking about: "Let your light shine so brightly that those around you who stand in the darkness will be illuminated by the light of who you really are."

Another one of the most critical aspects of coaching is to earn the respect of those around you. I don't believe a coach can gain respect unless he is consistent. If a coach always did different things in similar circumstances, the word consistency would not come to mind as appropriate. A coach who is constantly assuming a different perspective and changing the thought process keeps those around him guessing what comes next. Little good can come from something based on unexpected changes and inconsistencies.

Two things really shape and make a great team. That is balance and harmony. Balance to me, deals more with the physical side of things, while harmony is more of an emotional and behavioral factor.

Balance begins with having a team with the right mindset concerned with overall team strategy and tactics. Then a coaching staff's challenge is to offset the unequal abilities that exist on a team by assisting those with lesser abilities to work at practice on maximizing their strengths. In this regard, everyone on the team has the assurance they will possess the skills to give them a chance to compete.

Balance helps make for a better team. When every player works hard at improving himself and pushes his teammates to do the same, this results in the greater good. It never hurts to strive for balance.

Harmony creates a culture of togetherness. No one wants to play in a toxic environment. Harmony sets the foundation for future success by creating a culture where everyone has a pretty doggone good feel for their role and responsibility.

The message is plain: players and coaches alike need to blend in. We all know teamwork and working together as a unit are critical components in successful teams. However, that doesn't mean there are no disagreements and elements of friction on a team. A spirit of harmony means that teammates and coaches work through those moments and seek collaborative solutions when the locker room plays host to turmoil and disorder.

Finally, I want to say a few words about leadership. Blessed are those who are leaders. Strong leadership is needed to turn team goals into reality. The best leaders on a team, in my estimation, are the ones who lead by example. But I also think that effective leadership depends on utilizing good communication skills.

The thing is, it's not simple to develop leaders. All the great team leaders I had over the years had one thing in common: they directly impacted the team's success and ability to deliver results. You can't develop a winning team without having the right talent—including leaders—on the roster.

Some believe that great leaders are born. Others believe that leaders are made. The truth is, no manual or guide will give a player all the tricks to become a great leader. Being a leader comes through the maturation of wisdom that generally comes through experience and maturity. At least that has been my experience.

The bottom line is those players who are leaders play a critical role in the success of any team. These leaders have great ability in steering and encouraging others toward common goals. Blessed be the those who aspire to be leaders.

PART

IV

BETWEEN THE LINES

Chapter Thirteen

RISK TO GAIN

Talent used grows…talent ignored goes.

You know what you have done. You know how far you have come. But you don't know what you are capable of doing--you don't know how far you can go. While you cannot go back and make a brand-new start, you can start now and make a brand-new beginning. The ever-present challenge is to expand your horizons as if there are no limits to your potential. You begin to accept this challenge, when you choose to step out of your comfort zone and confront your fears. Only then can you effectively embark on the journey to move beyond what you are for the greater reward of what you can become.

Risk is to Step Beyond

To play is to risk losing…
To establish big goals is to risk exposure…
To perform before a crowd is to risk their ridicule…
To reach out to teammates is to risk involvement…
But to be a winner, risks have to be taken.
Taking risks is always a part of a winner's portfolio.
To have a chance to win…risk the chance of losing.

Risk is a four-letter word many potential elite athletes tend to approach with extreme caution. Risk in the sports world calls for anything but caution. It is necessary for growth. Risk is definitely inescapable and basically essential to being productive in athletics.

Taking measured risks is the price you must pay to make progress in virtually any sport. Athletes who are afraid to take even minimal risks may avoid the immediate pain that comes from doing just enough to get by, but they also forfeit the deep-felt sense of well-being that comes when they extend beyond the ordinary to seek the extraordinary.

Very little athletic potential is unleased when one waits for all the possible roadblocks to be removed before even beginning to stretch out toward a brighter future. While the future is always uncertain, the ability to engage even measured risks makes the future less uncertain than it otherwise would be.

Risk-taking is built on the premise that you can never have it any different than you have got it until you are willing to do something you have never done before. That means exploring new territory and expanding into something unknown--something that has not been part of your regular routine. It will be through your commitment of accepting the right kind of risks that will lead to the development of your talents, abilities and resources.

We want you to understand there are potential consequences when you do nothing, just as surely as there are consequences when you attempt something new and different--and have little to no success in the beginning.

Appreciate the fact it is far better to have the courage to act in an attempt to bring about better results, than to fail to act and end up on the short end of the stick. When you do your best regardless of the odds, at least you are making every effort to bring improvement to your play. This attitude alone will play well in the future.

"Winners tend to face the challenges before them
with a staff in their hands instead of a crutch."
-Dr. Tom White

Fear of Losing

The inability to take reasonable risk often has as its origin the thoughts created by fear of the consequences. Think about this: No one is afraid to try something new--they are afraid of the unknown that comes with it. No one is afraid of praise and adoration--they are afraid that they won't live up to it.

No one is afraid of sticking their neck out--they are afraid they won't like themselves if they are unsuccessful. No one is afraid to reach out to do something different--they are afraid they will not be liked if they do. No one is afraid of the future--they are afraid of what's in it. As someone said, "Fear kills more dreams than failure ever could."

Everything worth pursuing requires crossing a threshold of fear. It is an uncomfortable journey at times, but it is generally worth the effort. Whatever you do, don't let your fears determine your future. Everything you want out of athletics is on the other side of fear, but you must crossover the fear threshold to reach it.

It has been our experience those who tend to maximize their talents are not always right, but they are not fearful of being wrong. The reality of it is they tapped into their deepest resources and capacities and stepped away from their fears to do things they were formerly afraid to do. That's you, isn't it?

"Show me a team that has a fear of losing…and
I will show you a team that is easy to beat."
Geno Auriemma

Risk and opportunity are two sides of the same coin. In every opportunity there is risk. But it is equally true that in risk, there is the possibility of a great opportunity. Risk and opportunity walk hand-in-hand along the winners' path.

"Don't Strike Out Looking"

This baseball term has application for all sports. You see, nothing leads to a more miserable existence than being habitually indecisive when an important at-bat (decision) is at hand.

Probably the easiest decision we ever make is to not make a decision. Yet, when we decide not to decide, haven't we already decided? Being cautious when facing an important decision is not out of the norm, but we have to be careful not to choose the path of least resistance. Generally speaking, selecting whatever appears to be the easiest, or the safest choice, certain does little for advancement.

We can never have it any different than we have got it until we are willing to consistently swing the bat to obtain better results than we have been receiving. Baseball manager, Joe Maddon, provides another appropriate way to say it, "If you are going to strike out, do it swinging the bat. Don't leave the batter's box with the bat on your shoulder."

Indecision affects every athlete at some point and in some way, just as it does the baseball hitter. The inability to make a key, timely decisions not only mars the present, it dims the brightness of the future. "I wish I had only swung the bat…" is the hallmark of too many who failed to swing the bat in crucial situations.

Let's stay with our baseball analogies for additional reminders of the importance of "don't strike out looking." Babe Ruth offered this advice, "You cannot hit home runs unless you are willing to strike out." Added Ralph Houk, when he was the New York Yankee manager, "If you are afraid of striking out, the odds shift in favor of striking out."

The bottom line here is simple: Isn't it better to "swing the bat" (be decisive) and have a chance to obtain positive results, than to fail to "swing the bat" and get little done. When we perpetually have one foot in the air, we are never on sound footing.

"Advancing slowly is not a big detriment
to progress, but standing still is."
-Quimby Rogers

"Thus Far…No Farther"

Beethoven, the great music composer, had a favorite maxim: "The barriers are not yet erected which can say to aspiring talent and industry, 'thus far and no further'."

"Thus far and no farther" is what happens when we seek security at any cost…when there is no openness to experience…when we prefer to stick with doing things the same way--even after time and conditions suggest we should be doing something different.

Do you sense that we think moving beyond this attitude is important? We refer to setting aside the status quo many times. It is crucial you create a mindset that allows you to explore new possibilities and examine potential answers to sports most pressing questions. Habitual thought patterns become your reality when you constantly hold back and fail to keep searching for ways to improve.

Why is it so difficult being decisive when seeking better ways to perform? Instead of appreciating reality as it unfolds, the easier route to take is to continuously keep mulling over in your mind various options about what ought to be done. So long as you have one foot in the air, you are never on solid ground. The centerpiece to this thought pattern is you generally end up focusing on those things which possibly could go wrong, without greater thought as to a possible positive outcome.

This indecisive thought pattern will continuously repeat itself until you make the conscious decision to focus on creating movement leading to a systematic change in this inertia thought pattern. Your level of achievement will be enhanced simply by shifting your perspective toward being more actively engaged in exploring new ways to perform.

A body in motion tends to remain in motion. A body at rest will tend to remain at rest. Even then doing certain things may not come naturally and you may have to consciously train yourself to think about them until they become second nature. Just keep in mind that progress is rarely made until you are willing to stretch out and move beyond "thus far and no further." And don't forget: "What you take for granted and fail to use, will eventually disappear."

Be decisive. It is far better to make a decision and have a chance to get something done than to fail to make a decision and get nothing done. When you have confidence in your ability to make tough decisions, you give yourself a chance to perform at a higher level than you have ever performed at before.

Route to Progress

Hopefully, we have distinguished that few things in sports limits athletic prowess as much as the attitude of playing it safe. What presumably is a safe place is not necessarily a secure place. The only safe place that is going to be secure is not the place where we are right now. It's on up the road and when we arrive there, it will be even further up the road. Progress is always out front. It indicates we go where you have never been before.

A law of life reads: *"You either progress or regress, you don't stand still."* Elite athletes make progress by stepping out to venture beyond the familiar to engage the unknown. They have come to realize progress is stymied if they sit back and wait for something to happen, rather than to attempt to make something happen.

Progress is made when you are constantly working to expand your boundless potential. It involves constantly stretching and reaching. It is finding ways to continuously grow and develop. It is always believing there is a greater experience. Progress has at its very core the belief that until something is ventured, little is gained.

Hoping and wishing are not the watchwords of those who aspire to be champions. Champions are creators of favorable circumstances, not victims of bad circumstances. They are not imprisoned by security and comfortable habits. They are not trapped by routine. They do not cling to the familiar. They understand those who are not afraid to lose, always put themselves in a better position to win.

Follow Your "Doer"

A little later on in the book, you will find these words: "It takes no talent to be a quitter." Those who give up and quit at the first sign of difficulty while executing a new skill or technique are going against nature's grand design. In His great wisdom, our Creator planted a "doer" right in the pit of our stomachs that gnaws at us when we want to give up and quit, before giving something ample opportunity to work.

Regrettably, there are athletes that to save face don't necessarily fail, they simply don't try something that could improve their play. No one can fail at something until they try it, can they? They would rather run the risk of passing on an opportunity to enjoy potentially greater results, than to face the possibility they might not like themselves if they begin to do something and have little, or no, success. As a result, they don't fail...they just don't make the attempt.

If you feel this is being directed toward you, ask yourself if you are listening to your "doer?" When faced with the thoughts of giving up, tune in to that little gnawing sound coming from your "doer." From this vantage point, you will find yourself welcoming and accepting challenges you have not previously accepted. The future is always uncertain, but by listening to your "doer," you make the future less uncertain than it otherwise would be.

Another great tool that maximizes your "doer," is to draw energy and encouragement from the successful people around you. These are the ones who recognized a long time ago the real significance of acting on their "doer" with courage and conviction. These are the individuals who became unafraid to do things that they were formerly afraid to do.

Let Big Mo…Go

When you get your engine revered up and going, momentum has a chance of settling in. Once the surge starts, everything begins to click, making it hard to stop. Seriously, there is no law that says a good thing once started cannot be kept going until a goal is achieved. The old saying: "All good things must come to an end" is not a truism

...unless one quits doing all of the "good things" that created the momentum in the first place.

Winning is connected with taking the initiative and generating action. Successful athletes get in the swing of things and keep moving, building momentum as they go. What actions could you take today to produce better momentum for your career?

Say "No" to Yourself

Making mental adjustments often means you may have to give up something in order to establish a path toward something better. Learning how to say "No" to yourself is often the beginning of replacing old thought patterns with more positive thought patterns.

How good are you at saying, "No" to yourself? There is real value in learning to say "No" to those activities that could take you away from performance-enhancing opportunities.

The key to saying "No" is to learn to be a "self-boss," for the more you "boss" yourself from within, the less you will need to be "bossed" from without. If this is a challenge for you, get a real grip on managing yourself, or the time will come when you will have nothing else to manage. Make sense?

Learn to say 'No' to the unimportant things, so it is easier for you to get to the important 'Yesses' in your athletic career.

Nothing Average Ever...

Have you ever heard anyone say, "I really look forward to being average?" Not everyone will profess to wanting to be a super athlete. Excellent will be good enough for some. But no one wants to be average. Average is a term reserved for politicians, mathematicians and baseball hitters. Just keep in mind, that if you seek the average level you cannot hope to achieve a higher level of success...your only hope is to avoid being on the bottom level.

Nothing average ever stood as a monument to progress ...for when progress is looking for a partner, it doesn't turn to those who believe they are only average--it turns instead to those who are forever searching and striving to become the very best they possibly can be. Just keep in mind, elite athletes never think in terms of being average. Their goal is to always be the best that they possibly can be.

To Be Average

To be average is to seek security instead of opportunity... to let an endless string of opportunities to pass by... to accept the status quo as the best existence.

To be average is to be imprisoned by the comfortable habit of doing what one is required to do... not what one is capable of doing--to be less than what one can become.

To be average is never to perform at a higher level...to tune one's receiver to the mediocre frequency and join the pack...to adjust to the standards of others.

To be average is to be "the top of the bottom, the bottom of the top... the best of the worse, the worst of the best."

To be average is to have sat on the sidelines and accepted minimal risks and made minimal decisions in the most important game of all -- the game of life.

A SONNY MOMENT

Through the years, I have seen an enormous number of athletics with unlimited upside who failed to even come close to maximizing their potential. It is when you want to do something and have the ability to do something, but you fail to do something, that you end up bad mouthing yourself for not doing something. The simplistic question remains, why didn't you do something?

I going to speak to both coach and athlete in answering this question. The bottom line for a coach is winning. That means coaches must be good in developing raw talent into winning talent. But the ultimate development of talent rests with the individual player. I have seemed countless athletes who neither recognized nor appreciated their massive potential. As a coach I knew there was more--much more--these players were capable of doing. My job was to help them find out what was keeping them from being highly functional players..

I discovered over the years, it was often some type of fear that kept talented players from fulfilling their potential. One of the greatest facets of coaching is to convince underachievers that they have much greater capabilities available for them to work with. I think when players finally grasp they have what it takes to be elite performers, they feel safe enough to move beyond fear to show coaches what they are capable of doing. That is one of the top achievements that comes from coaching.

I must admit I was a "pusher." I probably pushed the more talented player harder than the less talented. Athletic success may have come too easy for that player because of his talent level. But the higher an athlete expects to climb, the more he will need to develop his overall skills. His athleticism will only get him so far. "Push. Push. Push." That in my way of thinking moves the needle for the talented player.

I think competitiveness enters into the picture in unleashing potential, as well. All athletes are competitive. But it has been my experience that there are different degrees of competitiveness. Those in the top echelon of that hierarchy, compete in all that they do.

The competitiveness of elite athletes extends far beyond a playing field or an arena. It is vitally important for them to do their best in whatever and wherever they compete. Simply put: They work to be number one in everything they do on the field and off.

The simplicity of sports is your success as an athlete can be traced to your own actions. It is within your power that you add to or detract from what happens in your future. So, what type of future you experience, to a large extent, lies within your own hands--in making something happen right now--right where you are. Translated: your future will be determined by the kind of initiatives you take now to unleashed your potential and move toward elite athletic status.

Start where you are. Do something that moves you. Do something that excites you. Don't talk about it. Don't dream about it. Don't keep planning for it. Just do it.

Chapter Fourteen

A LITTLE BIT MORE

Four short words sum up what lifts most
high caliber athletes above the crowd:

-A LITTLE BIT MORE-

They do all that is expected of
them…and then -- a little bit more.

One thing that helps champions become champions is they are constantly thinking about how to do a little more to make them better. They instinctively turn their attention not only to what needs to be done, but to what is yet to be done. They don't sit back and wait for something to come along to do…they go out and make something happen. They are always looking for—and working toward—doing ordinary things in an extraordinary way…not tomorrow, but right where they are now.

"A little bit more" attitude gives you a big edge in the way you feel about yourself. To get ahead, take advantage of those in charge by doing more than is asked or required of you…and keep doing it!!

"The road is sparsely populated along the extra mile."
-Josh Billings

Under Fire

Here's a great experiment to illustrate how various things differ "under fire." They very well could be indicative of how athletes differ when the heat is on.

Take a piece of meat, some sand, a clump of clay, a piece of wax, and some wood and throw all them into a fire. Now, how do suppose they will react? The meat fries...the sand dries up...the clay hardens...the wax melts...and the wood burns.

Every one of these items is acted upon by the same force--the fire. Yet, all reacted differently During the heat of an athletic contest, athletes react differently to the action before them. One may become stronger... another weaker...even another may do nothing. Which one is the most indicative of you? How do you react under fire?

Your wisest decision today is one where you do the things that will help you stretch out toward a better tomorrow. It is important to understand that every skill...every technique...every bit of knowledge you acquire...every thought you think, unites you with the future. What you do today is going to be a part of the rest of your career.

"One of the quickest ways to quit growing is to
make caution your number one form of exercise."
-Bill Battle

"Do not let what you cannot do
interfere with what you can do."
-John Wooden

Attentive Presence

If you take a good look at the term "a little bit more," the whole process of going the extra mile begins with thinking in terms of doing best where you are right now. The focus is on wherever you are and at whatever you are doing at that very moment you are thinking, "What do I need to do right now to do this a little bit better?"

Sometimes you have to overcome a tendency to wait for conditions to be a little better before you make a strategic move. However, often in athletics, you have to do your best with less than the best. Rarely will you always have the best of everything to work with, but you can make the best of everything that is available for you to work with. That is a result of a "Do a little bit more" attitude.

Our recommendation is don't wait until you have more time...until you feel more comfortable...until you are in a better position. Just get after it, starting where you are–just as you are. Simply put, be willing to do your best with conditions as you find them, even if conditions are not the best. The rule: Make the best of less than the best, for what guarantee do you have that conditions or circumstances will be any better later.

Take to heart these great suggestions to "be wherever you are:"

- The most effective and efficient way to get things done is to "wherever you are…be there."
- Whatever gets your attention gets you.... for wherever your focus, that's where your heart will be.
- Focus on each play as it happens… and you will always be in touch with the present.
- When your attention is centered around the things that you should be doing, the things that can go right, your actions will reflect this positive "compete to win' attitude… and that's the direction in which your play will take you.
- Absorb yourself in the present action. Then a prior mistake or setback does not fracture your approach ...because you know it was only temporary.
- Winners forget about trying to do everything that needs to be done at once -- but focus on doing the one thing that needs to be done at once.
- When you focus on the task at hand, you are less sensitive to the "negatives" around you, the kind of things that work against a "do a little bit more approach.

- Your best chance is where you are right now... for what you might consider to be "no chance" may well turn out to your only chance to contribute to your team's success.
- If you focus 10% of your energy and intentions on 10 things, then you rarely get anything worthwhile done. Again, don't forget the monotasking rule: focus on one thing at once.
- Those who lose focus--lose. Direct all of your energy toward doing all that is expected of you—then you are in position to do even more.

"A great reputation is never built on what you are going to do. Do it and see how many others like it."
-Earl Miller

Keep working to perform at a higher level--because a higher level is just one step or performance away."
-Ben Sweetland

"Don't wear your wishbone where your backbone ought to be."
-Adolph Rupp

"Around here backbone has proven to have a better return on time invested than does wishbone."
-Frank Howard

"It is not the critic who counts, nor the man who points out how who knows great enthusiasm, great devotion and the triumph of achievement and who, at the strong man stumbles or where the doer of deeds could have done better. The credit belongs to the man who is actually in the arena, whose face is marred by dust and sweat and blood; the worst, if he fails, at least fails while doing greatly-so that his place shall never be with those cold and timid souls who know neither victory nor defeat."
-President Theodore Roosevelt

DO what needs to be done.
DO it when it needs to be done.
DO it the very best you know how to do it.
DO it that way every time you are doing it.
-Unknown source

The key to being a consistently excellent performer is to never save your best performance for tomorrow… because the tomorrow you are saving your best performance for will end up looking just like yesterday's performance. Your best security for performing better tomorrow is to give your all today and let tomorrow take care of itself.

When you are worth your salt,
you make others thirsty."
--Nolin Richardson

To be bigger tomorrow start acting today with "a little bit more" attitude. It is important that you perform with the confident expectation of what is to come--to answer with an unqualified "yes" the challenges you face in the classroom…at the practice facility…during a game—and then you will be in a position to do a little bit more.

It is great to plan ahead…to visualize a course of action…to set future goals and think in terms of future results. But the key to the future is what happens in the present, isn't it? Success is built around the ability to focus on the NOW…that puts you in a great position to succeed in the present.

Strive for Excellence

One of the biggest challenges for young athletes is the feeling they should be perfect. But perfectionism is not a realistic standard. Athletes who expect perfection have a tendency to spend valuable time thinking up excuses for why things got off track, or thinking of ways to cover up mistakes. Perfectionists never give themselves a license for being anything but perfect.

Being a perfectionist places the spotlight on feelings that you are never good enough. Typically, the rigidness of a perfectionist attitude leads to your finding it difficult to let go of a misplay or error on your part. This unwavering approach magnifies the consequences of not playing well. The results then are very predictable: your play can become even worse.

Consistently good performances require cutting yourself some slack and making an effective compromise with perfection. Focus on being less self-critical. Don't become so upset when you make a mistake...miss a "sure bet"...drop the ball...or even occasionally come out on the short end of the stick.

Being more flexible in your thought process is also important. Counter those perfectionistic thoughts with positive self-talk (discussed earlier in chapter six). You don't have to be perfect to be a top-notch athlete; excellence is good enough.

Strive for excellence all the time…for excellence is a habit--not a sometimes act.

"The key to a team's success is to chase perfection and catch excellence."
-Tom Landry

A SONNY MOMENT

One of the things I learned rather quickly in coaching is that doing things that end up being the wrong way offers an opportunity to learn what is the right way. That goes for coaches and athletes alike. I mean if you are unwilling to do things because you are afraid to fail, you will do little toward reaching out to do the things that will move the needle toward being a champion.

While I think it is important for players to play within themselves, that doesn't mean they shouldn't ever take a chance. Players who have a real feel for their own playing characteristics, know their assignments inside and out, and how a really good feel for their own capabilities, are the ones who are less likely to be afraid of failing.

I didn't have a problem with a player acting spontaneously here and there who had built a solid reputation with his coaches and teammates because of his steady and guided play. All coaches seek an element of predictability from their players, but predictability can have a comfort level that thwarts creative and daring play… sometimes when it is most needed.

There is something else which tends to hold players back. It is a habitual thought pattern of indecisiveness. I see as the centerpiece of this thought pattern the tendency to focus on what can go wrong, without proper thought to a possible positive outcome. An indecisive thought pattern can become the master of your destiny and will repeat itself continuously until you make a conscious effort to trust yourself and become more decisive in your decision-making.

Your level of achievement as an athlete can be enhanced simply by a shift in your perspective to being more actively engaged in doing something that gets you moving toward creating positive action. A body in motion tends to remain in motion. A body at rest will tend to remain at rest. What gets the body moving is the conscious decision to create movement that leads to a systematic change in this thought pattern. That's something you can consciously bring about…if you will.

Chapter Fifteen

HANGING TOUGH

Hanging tough is cut from the fabric of persistence and woven with perseverance. There are no areas in athletics immune to this combination…you will go as far as your stay-ability will allow you to go.

Plan for Adversity

Imagine what it would be like if you went through your life never encountering any adversity or any other obstacles for that matter? That might sound good, but we all know it is not realistic. The very struggles you face in life make you the person you become. If you are not tested nor face resistance, how do you grow?

The same is true in sports. If your basic outlook accepts that unusual things of a negative nature are a natural part of sports, this will undoubtedly make you more mentally prepared when adversity does arise. How you view adversity is crucial. Without a certain degree of tolerance and understanding of adverse situations, they can appear to be eternal and never ending.

Murphy's Law says, "When something can go wrong, a time will arise when it will." For many of us, when the occasion occurs where something adverse happens, it comes as a shock creating an extreme mental uneasiness. The depth of the feelings experienced when things get out of whack depends on how ready we are for its occurrence.

Plan. Prepare. Practice. That's the route to being ready for things which can get off track. Practice time is the time to spend in preparation what might go wrong and other unexpected occurrences that can arise during play. Your mind will be much more capable of handling adverse situations when you do everything possible to acquaint yourself with them. Secondly, mentally think of adversity as a challenge that you are always ready to take on.

Adversity has a way of defining you, depending on how you stand up to it. It also offers the potential to refine you and make you better as you work your way through it. Not around, but through.

> "It is easy to jump to the conclusion that something is over when things look bleak, isn't it? Yet an essential part of developing a champion's mentality, is to hang in there when the going gets tough and success appears out of sight."
>
> Dr. Ken Blanchard

"If it is worth doing, it is worth doing wrong."
-Tom Peters

"You are what you are when the going gets tough."
-Yogi Berra

"Tough times never last, but tough people do."
-Knute Rockne

To never admit making mistakes enhances the chances of making them again.

"Adversity does not define you,
but what happens when it strikes will."
-Bill Walton

"Tough sledding is an opportunity for
growth…not an excuse for giving up."
Dr. Wayne Dyer

Sometimes you can get knocked off your feet by something beyond your control. but when you get knocked down, the responsibility still falls to you to get up. Remember no one is ever a loser by getting knocked down...they only become a loser if they don't get back up--and then do whatever it takes to stay up!

"Don't get discouraged. when things have gone about as wrong as they can go. Hang in there--stay the course--and you will emerge on the other side a wiser and stronger ballplayer."

-Fred Hatfield

There will always be something from previous action left within you. Each new beginning carries with it a lesson from things that have happened to you in the past.

"An eraser is not for those who make mistakes…
it is for those willing to correct their mistakes."
-Source unknown

"Something outside of you can stop you
temporarily, only you can do it permanently."
-Frank Beamer

"Bad things which struck are meant to instruct."
-Benjamin Franklin

No Challenges…No Glory

Great progress emerges from great challenges.

Here's the big question: How good are you at hanging in there when the going gets tough and the outcome is unclear? Does this type of challenge draw out the very best within you?

Challenges in any phrase of athletics give you glimpses of yourself that you may have never seen. They give you a chance to see your make up. They can rush to your aid qualities which you may have never known you possess. Challenges simply give you a chance to be better than you have ever been…if you face up to them.

A truism in sports is there is no measure of gain without pain...no triumphs without trials...no victories without battles...no peaks without valleys…no glory without challenges. Speaking of valleys, Coach Bobby Bowden reminds us that, "The fertilizer that helps us do our best growing is found in the valley, not on the mountaintop."

If you have built strong habits of persistence, and of mental discipline, you will be aided by these virtues when you face tough challenges. If you have prepared yourself to face up to challenging situations with courage and conviction --the chances are good that you will enjoy significant rewards. It is worth noting that the challenges you face and work to overcome today are developing the courage and strength which makes tomorrow's challenges easier to face.

To overcome a difficult challenge doesn't create a "hero," it just brings to the surface the hero that is already present.

A real factor in winning is the ability to
hang on where others tend to let go.
A more significant factor is your ability
to hang on when you want to let go.
-Source unknown

"It is easy to jump to the conclusion that something is over when things look bleak, isn't it? Yet an essential part of developing a champion's mentality, is to hang in there when the going gets tough and success appears out of sight."

-Les Brown

The Real Test

The test of any athlete is the fight he makes,
The grit that he daily shows;
The way he stands on his feet and takes
The opponent's toughest blows;
Anyone can do well when there's nothing to fear,
When nothing his progress bars;
But it takes a real athlete to stand and cheer
When someone else stars.
The sweet taste of victory comes after all,
To the athlete who can make
A courageous stand with his back to a wall;
The one who can give and take,
And always hold his head up high –
Even when bruised and pale;
For this is the athlete who will always try,
Because he's not afraid to fail.
It is when you decide to make a stand –
And you have courage to remain
Strong when victory is almost at hand,
That will decide if you win the game.
For the real test of your mettle and worth
Is to fight just one more round.
And ultimately, how you do in the arena,
Is decided by standing your ground.
--Adapted from an Unknown Source

"You will always perform at a high peak when you discipline yourself to focus on doing your best every time you have an opportunity, as if it were going to be the first—and the last time you will ever see it."
-Tony Robbins

Keep going even when quitting
would appear the most likely choice.
-Bob Henderson

Too Soon to Quit

Some have told you it can't be done,
Maybe you have thought them right;
But the time will come to move ahead,
Because somehow you think you might.
In the beginning losses may be too many,
Putting to the supreme test your grit;
But a little voice will say: "Stay with it,
Hang in there, it's too soon to quit!"
So, you raised your sights a bit higher,
And charged up with a brand-new will;
You dug your heels in a little deeper,
Because you have big dreams to fulfill.
Then the day arrived to your surprise,
You did what others said couldn't be done;
For you had learned it's too soon to quit,
And with that attitude, by golly you won! -
Adapted from an unknown author

"The toughest person to beat, is the one
who doesn't know the meaning of quit."
-Jim Valvano

"Today's mighty oak is yesterday's
little nut who held its ground."
-Josh Billings

G.rit

U.nder

T.ough

S.ledding

"The greatness of an individual's strength is the
measure of that individual's tendency to surrender."
-General George Patton

"When you think you have done all you can and want to give in; Please be reminded that winners don't quit, and quitters don't win."
-Source Unknown

"Remember the person who gave up? Neither does anyone else."
-Bud Grant

"There is no defeat except within; unless you are defeated there, you'll find a way to win."
-William Danforth

"We can keep going long after we think we can."
- Lou Gehrig

"You have to love the person whose heart is bursting with a passion to overcome."
-Gordie Howe

It takes a lot of heart, nerve and fortitude to hang in there when things go very wrong, and you have very little to cling to, except a little voice telling you to "HOLD ON!"
-Source unknown

"Nothing in the world can take the place of persistence. Talent will not; nothing is more common than unsuccessful men with talent. Genius will not: unrewarded genius is almost a proverb. Education will not: the world is full of educated derelicts. Persistence and determination alone are omnipotent."
-Unknown source

Persistence is the ability to keep going when you need to keep going, after you think you have done about all you can do.

Deep down on the inside you are not a quitter...you don't give up at the first sign of trouble…you are willing to deny yourself easy exits because you know you have what it takes to hang tough. You know if you keep working and keep believing, you will emerge on the other side stronger and wiser and know what it is like to overcome any adversity or any challenge.

Keep Yogi Berra's great quote in mind:

"It ain't over until it's over."

A SONNY MOMENT

Anyone who's ever played sports for any length of time knows there is never a time when you "throw in the towel" and start thinking about the next game. Winners don't give up until the final whistle blows or the match is over. Play every point, play, or down like it matters. Keep fighting—even if losing seems inevitable.

So, never give in, regardless of the score. Keep playing as hard and efficient as you possibly can. When you give up, you regret it afterwards…and if it is a contact sport, you are more accessible to injury. The fewer concessions you make to any opponent, the better you are going to feel about yourself going forward.

When you "throw in the towel" and begin to just go through the motions, you forfeit any chance for victory. I saw this over the years, a team is more apt to quit when they are the team favored to win, and find themselves hopelessly behind on the score. Players become frustrated and upset with what has happened, and fail to keep a forward-looking approach that might lead to a big rally and possibly pulling out a win.

Comebacks happen. Opponents can get complacent with a big lead and start making mistakes. If a team continues to play hard and aggressive, it could be the catalyst that leads to snatching victory from the jaws of defeat. The point is you never know what might happen if you keep scrambling and fighting so long as there is time still left on the play clock. Believe me, elite athletes know all about big comebacks and underdogs defeating heavily favored opponents.

Chapter Sixteen

FAIL (LOSE) FORWARD

Admirable as the ideal of winning every time is, no one can win them all. Losing happens…but what counts when a team loses is how team members mentally react to losing.

The price is high. because what each player on the team thinks after they have experienced a loss is often the determining factor in how long it takes to disconnect from the loss, and bounce back.

Before a team can learn what consistently winning is all about, it must first learn how to lose. It must learn how to quickly bounce back after a loss—notably one where everyone on the team knew they should have won.

> "Failure can be defined as a wrong that leaves an impression that turns you in toward yourself. To come up on the short end of the score has no consequences going forward, unless you let it deter you from moving on to the next challenge."
>
> Dr. Bob Everhart

Winners are not the ones who shy away from losing, nor the ones who never lose...but rather the ones who move forward--who go on in spite of setbacks, learning all the while the lessons that minimizes the chances of losing…again.

"The first thing that should come from losing is the feeling that you don't like it."
-Woody Hayes

Untangle the Tangled

Life is full of difficulties, setbacks and missteps. So is athletics. One of the things that will help you reach elite athlete status is to learn how to untangled the tangled of sports. Mentally, you see the difficulties you faced as stepping stones rather than stumbling blocks.

One of the first things you can do to untangle the tangled is to let go of those less-than-successful moments experienced in the past. Elite athletes have learned how to strip away all the accumulative layers of negative things that have happened a

Of course, you still remember those bad events. There's nothing wrong with simply remembering those negatives that were part of your past; but remembering them and dwelling on them are two different things. The key is how to put those memories in storage.

Elite athletes have discovered the past has passed, so there is no use continuing to mull it over in the mind. Nothing can be done to change what has happened, but there is definitely something that can be captured from it to brighten the future.

How about you? Do you think of the basic and essential premise of the positive benefits and lessons setbacks can almost certainly provide? Within each negative event is the innate potential of something really good. It may be hidden, but it is there. The challenge is to unfold the great treasures of potentiality that lies within the "negatives."

Once you have a handle on how you can benefit from the past, then you can move on to the next level in your growth and development. Discard the misstep, setback or loss. It is a thing of the past. Time to move on. Time to stretch out and reach a new level of growth.

Okay. How do you untangle the tangled? You must trust your own nature to untangle where you may have been all tangled up thinking of the "negatives" in the past. There are two things you need to do with the past: learn from it, then run from it.

Tough times are only as meaningful
as your memories of them.

"Forgettery"

Did you and your teammates do everything in your power to secure a win, and didn't? What happens now? The suggestion would be to let it hurt for a while--feel the sting, learn the lesson—then move on.

Sometimes it's the moving on part that is difficult. The secret of moving on is to let things come and go, by using your "forgettery" to move on to the next challenge. Your "forgettery" is one of the greatest weapons you can possess in the ability to forget and go on to what's next. This doesn't mean you are suppressing things or being carried away by them, but doing the best you can to learn from the situations, and then get ready for the next opponent or challenge.

Yet, isn't there a tendency to keep thinking about what should have been done or could have been done to win? Anytime a bad performance remains front and center in your thoughts, there is a good chance that it will affect the next performance…and then the next.

Earlier we distinguished after a loss, it's not what happened that becomes the biggest concern, it's what the team members think of what has happened. A team's weak moments are only strong as each team members memories of them.

A real outcome of having a good "forgettery," is it conserves mental energy. Total concentration on what's to come is not easy if the thought process remains on what has happened in the past. This results in mental tiredness, which makes you increasingly more prone to greater mistakes and lack of success.

Utilizing your "forgettery" helps to keep things on an even keel, neutralizing the tendency of emotional swings. It leads to a greater balanced approach, where the past is put into the past.

Winning the mental struggle after any losing situation centers in great part around having a good "forgettery." Those teams with members who have the best "forgettery," enjoy a greater degree of success than those who failed to stay focus on the now moment.

"Setbacks were meant to define…not defeat."

-Og Mandino

Recovery Capacity

Hopefully, we have distinguished that failure to do something that should have been done or could have been done is a great learning force. Obviously, that depends on being up to the task of learning from it, and then applying what you have learned to produce better future results.

Winning develops in an environment where a team maximizes its use of its forgettery, then engages in utilizing the power of its recovery capacity. Recovery capacity centers on a team's ability to bounce back by focusing on the "teachable moment" losing creates. A unified recovery capacity results in more productive efficiency going forward for both individual players and the team as a whole. The sustainability of the recovery depends in great part on the resiliency of the team.

The key element of a team's recovery capacity is the focus is not on what has happened, but what can happen. Lessons to be learned occur quickly and more readily when a team's recovery capacity is open to constructive instruction. Through this openness, a team is more capable of learning what it takes to win, then move on to the next game with increased vigor and mental acumen.

Moving beyond a loss, begins with controlling the one aspect of losing that is in each participant's hands… controlling their own thoughts about the loss.

"You will never be a winner acting like a loser...and the more comfortable you become with losing, the easier losing is."
-Nick Saban

"Things work out for the best when you make the best of the way things work out."
-Pat Head Summit

Loser's Limp

Anyone who has competed in sports for any length of time knows what a "loser's limp" looks like. For those who may not have heard the term "loser's limp," it is where a player acts out an injury after blowing a big play or failing miserably against a lesser opponent.

We would like to have a dollar for every time we saw this through the years; a player has a chance to score a big goal, and misses. He then begins to limp in "pain," looking for the crowd to say, "*Goodness gracious, he would have surely scored but for that injury.*"

Maybe the fans genuinely believed he has an injury, but what about the player himself? How about his teammates? The player knows by feigning an injury, he may manage to save face in front of the fans. They possibly believe his inability to perform at a peak level was because of the injury, but deep down the player himself knows better--he knows he blew it.

A player who employs a *"loser's limp,"* loses the respect of his coaches and teammates, notably when it becomes a fairly consistent occurrence. But the fact remains the player simply didn't execute when the chips were down.

We would venture that it is really human to want to provide rationale for poor performance by placing the blame on something or someone else. It happens to coaches, as well as individual players. How many referees or umpires have been blamed for a lost? That is always a convenient excuse, isn't it? It is still a "loser's limp" in our book.

We all fail to execute on occasion. Yet, if something on the outside is always responsible when things get off track, there is little desire and ambition to truly address the internal challenges. How about you? Do you tend to search for a crutch when you come up short?

To use the ready-made excuse of a "loser's limp," never changes the outcome. It never makes anything better, either. It has been our experience that the further up the success ladder a team or an athlete climb, the less they use a "loser's limp" as an excuse for poor results.

A couple of questions: If a team and individual players are never accountable for their shortcomings, how can they bring about improvement? What is there to improve on if a team is not willing to forego excuses for poor performances and make workable adjustments?

The rule is simple: "If you mess up, fess up." You can never find a solid step on the winners' ladder if you spend time searching for excuses. In order to move on beyond a "loser's limp," ask yourself this question: "What am I doing about the one thing I can improve: What am I doing about me?"

> "You will rarely *find* a place on the leaderboard, if you are always searching for excuses for poor performance or mistakes. A loser's limb is the forerunner to losing."
> -Arnold Palmer

> Nothing inhibits progress more than making excuses and passing the blame. The moment a team searches for an excuse--any excuse--is the moment that team limits its possibilities for future success. Relying on excuses for shortcomings, does nothing to change those faults. Please understand, the further up the success ladder a team hopes to climb, the less it will search for—and make-- excuses for poor performance.

Fail (Lose) Forward

The one thing that sets champions apart is their ability to use setbacks to do their best growing. They maintain this supportive feeling even if they give their best effort and come up short. It gives them more determination to right the ship and seek the next challenge. The lessons taught by those occasions when they have a lack of success is the driving force helping champions to refine and strengthen efforts going forward.

Here are some "fail forward" thoughts:

- Failure is simply a mental process…a state of mind.
- To admit that you were less than your best, is a sign of strength–not a confession of weakness.
- Don't ever talk like a failure—failure is certain then.

- Think: "When a team fails, it doesn't make it a failure. It is just a learning experience...and nothing more."
- A team will best be remembered by the times it succeeds--not by the times it failed.
- When a team comes up short, it is important that players not personalize it and put themselves down. A team wins together. A team loses together. The best policy is to always try to *"separate you from what you do."*
- Let the past -- pass. A lost only affects the next opportunity when the team holds on to the last poor one.
- Always "fail forward." Never look at a failure or loss in any other way than as a fulcrum for learning—that will facilitate coming out on the other side even smarter than before.

> "You can think about ways to win or ways to keep from losing. While the former does not always guarantee winning, the latter pretty much guarantees losing."
>
> -Bum Phillips

Fail Forward Process

Grasp the fact that to be successful, every team participant and coach must make losing a breeding ground where everyone learns what it takes to be turn failure into success. Since losing in the enactment of winning is a given, it is important that a team strive to fail forward.

The "fail forward" process involves three very distinct stages:

1. AWARENESS STAGE. "I should not be doing... (whatever needs to be done differently)."
2. ACCEPTANCE STAGE. "I should be doing... (options of what you should be doing)."
3. ACTION STAGE. "I will... (specify what you will do to bring improvement to your performance)."

What counts when a team loses is how team members react to losing. The price is high, because it is not the regrettable loss that carries the highest value, but the thought process you and your teammates have about the loss. The key factor is how long it takes for the team to mentally recover and get back on the road toward preparing for the next opponent.

A real understanding of what happened after it happened, provides a path to learn those thing which enable you to make something more promising happen.

"The road to success always has detour signs along the traveling route. This makes it a long try-way, not an easy road way."

-Zig Ziglar

Heads...Up

So, you lost. Got the stuffing knocked out of you, did you? What is your normal posture after you experience defeat? Head down with shoulders slumped, right? The head position is body language personified. Here is a great reminder: "Let me see your eyes."

Do you realize it's mentally impossible to walk around thinking negatively with your head up and eyes open? To think negatively, you have to drop your head, or even close your eyes. Head down is the position where you begin to think about all the "bad things" that have happened to you, or you envision will happen.

Every emotion has its corresponding physical counterpart. When you lift your head, square your shoulders and place your body erect, something great happens. These very physical acts trigger biological processes that alter the mind's perception of what it is "supposed to feel." You begin to think positive thoughts and feelings.

Keep your head up and eyes level, when things are not going your way. This simple act will serve to help you focus on what lies ahead. It will keep you positively focused on doing your best right where you are. You will find yourself making greater strides when your head is up and your eyes are open.

> "During any competitive event, a team should always perform in such a way that if it fails to come out on top, every member of that team should walk away feeling like the competitors succeeded more than they failed."
>
> -Dr. Marv Levy

> The (team) cannot go back again to the place where it started and make a brand-new beginning … but the (team) can start where it is now and make a brand-new ending."
>
> -Stephen Covey

Winning is never final; losing is never fatal.

Winning Gives Clues

This chapter has distinguished how important it is to learn the lessons arising from defeat. We are going to close this chapter talking about winning and the clues it affords as well for bringing about improved performance.

What do you and your teammates need to do to continue the climb up the success ladder in the fashion you have been demonstrating? Winning always has built in clues as to what must be done to continue along that path. There are lessons in winning just like there are in losing. The key is to look at winning as a building block…you will always find signs in winning that point out ways that will help to improve the process to enjoying successful results on a continuous basis.

Regardless of how high you and your teammates are on the success ladder, there are always things to learn to help make you better. You must constantly be evolving and improving your body of work.

A SONNY MOMENT

There are learning opportunities when you win as well as lose. Here's my rule: When you lose, learn from it. When you win, learn from it. Show up every day ready to improve.

While winning is important, not losing may be more important. Think about that a minute. You see losing engenders negative feelings and consequences, and given enough time and pressure lead to a general downward spiral of a team. In some situations, it often leads to the same within a community. For better or worse, sports have become that important in communities all across the country.

My feeling is that the first priority is to find ways to keep from losing. Elsewhere in the book you will find this quote, "The best thing that should come from losing is the feeling you don't like it." When that kind of attitude permeates a team, it has taken a step toward finding ways to keep from losing.

Developing a winning culture is no easy task. Winning is by design, not by accident. The road to both winning (and losing for that matter) is always under construction. Recognizing that, the architect of a winning culture will produce a very different route to travel on. That route begins with concentrative attention to a positive environment of words and actions.

Positivity has been the focus in this book. The insight in these pages sustain and further reflect upon the continuous flow of positive-building activity which portrays winning, not only as a destination, but as a journey. In that regard, every moment, every minute, every hour, every day a coach or player is involved in an athletic endeavor, the focus is on developing a winning culture.

Pay attention to everything that is happening right now with consciously heightened awareness. A winning culture may not come immediately—it rarely doe. It may only look like a good idea. But there is opportunity--there is possibility--if you are focusing on the moment before you.

These words are probably have more meaning to the players, but everyone associated with a team should understand the key factor in winning is encoded in the here and now. It is always now that you should be thinking about doing what it takes to be a winner. Not earlier, not later, not yesterday, not tomorrow, but right now. Center your attention to fully and completely invest this moment with your total focus on winning thoughts, as if it were your only moment. Winning is a consequence of a now thing. It is in the present that you build a more favorable foundation going forward.

While now is the result of all your yesterdays and the basis of all your tomorrows, the wise decision is to put the past behind you. In this chapter, we have talked about the importance of having a good "forgettery." Appreciate that you are the result of your past, but it is your present actions and words that have implications for the future. Your ability to move on is dependent on keeping the present front and center.

For the "here and now" team, a brighter future is on the horizon. It may not have arrived yet, but it is on its way. The only ground anyone associated with a team can stand on is the present. Even contemplating the future or the past is a function of present awareness. Lean heavily on that part of you that visualizes the possible instead of the impossible. An important step in this process is found in seeking more creative ways of expanding awareness. Awareness is what will allow any of us to come alive to the greatness we have within.

When awareness is small, we think small. We think in terms like, "I want to do enough to just get by." But when you enlarge your awareness, you explore in greater depth your unique gifts that are just waiting for you to awaken. You imagination expands in broader terms like: "I wonder just how good I can be?"

So, to me athletic success is about being aware of making progress from practice to practice, from game to game. As we know, a team may not be successful at all times, but with the right kind of mindset, it can always keep working to improve fundamentals and mechanics—the backbone things necessary for improved play.

Another key factor in a team's ability to consistently play at a high level is found in team leadership. Leadership requires good instincts from the more experienced players interacting with the other players. Leaders are those who are able to interact with other teammates in a positive way with a positive mindset. These leaders enhance the team's effort with thoughtful and effective words of instruction, inspiration and encouragement.

Player leadership is not bestowed, it is earned. It is not the role of team leaders to tell other players what they are not doing or can't do. The purpose of team leaders is to lift players up, not tear them down. The real leaders on a team are aware of how being positive leads to positive results—more often than not.

****

Before we go on, let me say something about when a team is winning and everything is going the right way. A coach may have to take the necessary steps to avoid an air of arrogance and haughtiness that can creep into a locker room. If you are not careful, the team can get too cocky and over-confident by good fortune, just as much so as by being less excited and lacking in self-confidence, by the bad. Keeping a team on an even keel is a constant thing, notably when the team is learning how to win.

I probably practiced my teams a tad harder when we were on a winning streak than when we were not enjoying a higher level of success. I often thought that losing was more apt to occur after a big win, so I preached we should take the path that focused on practicing harder than normal.

What I hope you hear me saying is winning ways easily can be reversed unless a team is constantly aiming higher...breaking through new barriers...using more productive ways to perform…striving for winning results every time they enter a competitive event or take on a new challenge. The record book is full of teams who let their press clippings get in the way of quality results.

A given in sports is that those with more drive and ambition will knock a team right off its pedestal if they are not working hard to get better. So, regardless of where a team is on the success ladder, no one--coaches or players alike--can ever afford to feel like they can just show up and win. A realism of competition is that a team with more desire and purpose will knock the cockiness right out of a team full of themselves, dropping them right down on their knees. I know from experience. I have been there.

Just for the record, please understand that winning is never final and losing is never fatal. Keep on striving toward being on the winning side of the score card.

***If you feel like you have had enough,
just look how far you have come.***

Chapter Seventeen

GAME-CHANGERS

ATTITUDE: assures how well you perform…time-after-time.

COMMITMENT: is about choosing to believe that what you are doing is the thing you highly desire doing. You believe it so unequivocally that there is no Plan B.

COURAGE: decides the extent to which you will stick your neck out to make something exciting happen.

DESIRE: determines how badly you want to be a champion. It's that inside flame only success can extinguish… momentarily.

ENDURANCE: describes the ability of the body to sustain athletic performance over an extended period of time.

ENTHUSIASM: sets the tone for the high level you use as you go about performing during training, practice or a game.

PERSISTENCE: sets the stage for how long you will continue the quest of seeking a successful conclusion without giving up.

RESILIENCY: establishes how well you bounce back from a setback to set the course toward the next challenging opportunity.

SELF-CONFIDENCE: demonstrates the inner feeling you are worthy of succeeding in any situation.

WILL TO PREPARE: determines how you go about preparing to become a champion.

Attitude

Here's that word "attitude" again. Developing a winning attitude is the first and vital step to winning the "head game." It is crucial to the level of your individual play that you have a healthy, ongoing attitude toward obtaining the results that helps put your team on the W side.

When you focus energy on the kind of results you want and expect, the brain is treated to an injection of *dopamine*. This is the chemical that makes us look forward to repeating winning experiences. Think about that: A healthy mental attitude toward winning influences the actions that lead to obtaining those results. Each time you anticipate you can obtain quality results, you are more apt to be endowed with the resources necessary for achieving those positive results.

No doubt a results-oriented attitude, will lead you in a winning direction. You will tend to see opportunities where other players fail to see them. It will be a guiding light in helping you to develop the fortitude to move through and over obstacles that possibly would stop less winning-oriented players.

Never underestimate the role your personal attitude plays toward the results the team obtains. Winning is the accumulation of a team's collective thoughts, attitude, and efforts. Winning is the ultimate barometer by which all things in athletics are measured.

Two Winning Ends

You have two winning ends,
They have a common link…
With the bottom end you move…
With the top end you think.
And winning truly depends on
How you maximize their use;
For common sense dictates–
With both you win--one you lose.
-Adapted from an unknown author

You are your attitudes and your attitudes are you.

Commitment: The Soul of Winners

The quality of your athletic experience will be in direct proportion to your commitment to being an elite athlete. Commitment is about choices, not conditions. Commitment helps you fight through any impediments that could keep you from any goal.

Nothing great is ever accomplished without commitment to the process that has been proven to be successful. Commitment is the common denominator among those who become consistent winners—it requires a heart and soul effort–and you can only put your heart and soul into something you are committed to doing with your whole being.

Commitment is about choosing to believe that something can be done better. It is about choosing to believe that you can succeed. The more committed you are to accomplishing something, the more likely you are to find a way to make it a reality. Inspired by a commitment to succeed makes tough situations to appear less difficult and more doable.

The source for commitment arises deep within your very being. Innate talent isn't what will place you among the best, rather it is simply the commitment you have for maximizing your talent. To say it another way, "Your skills and abilities won't get you up in the morning, but your commitment to be an elite athlete will."

If you are committed, then you are driven by something far deeper than interest. Being driven is a gut reaction to an intense internal craving. It works its way down through the creases and grooves to settle quietly into the corners of your whole being.

Check on your commitment. Are you super committed to becoming an elite athlete? Get the commitment factor right—first. Once it is solidified, it becomes the core of your passion for being special.

Commitment centers around a WILL DO attitude, for when WILL DO shows up—HOW TO is not far behind.

Pass-I-on

Establishing a deep-felt passion for what you are doing sets right at the heart of commitment. It is this passion that sparks the desire to want to be committed – to be locked in to doing your best. Passion keeps you going and growing, for it is through passion that you answer the question: "How can I do better?"

Your desire to become something special as an athlete, arises out of a passion to become the best you possibly can be. To reach this worthy goal, you have to be willing to passionately give of yourself in order to receive something for yourself…and the passion comes first.

When you feel passionate about the activity before you, there is no great difference between the way you perform in practice and the way you perform during a game. You work tirelessly to make the best of every practice and game opportunity. You are dedicated to being satisfied with only your best effort--regardless.

Passion is nurtured from the inside out. It originates in a heart that yearns to ride the winds of adventure. It is the key to thriving. Others may not remember your exact actions, but they will remember the passion you demonstrated in your actions. Is your PASS-I-ON worth passing on?

"A vision for the future arises from
your passion…not your position."
-Dr. John Maxwell

"There is a significant difference between being interested in something and being passionate about it. When you are interested in something, you work at it only when it is convenient. When you are passionate about something, you go about doing it with all your being."

Dr. Ken Blanchard

Never leave your best effort in the locker room. Develop a passion for going all out, all the time.

Courage

"Courage is not the lack of fear, it is the conquest of it."
-William H. Danforth

The opposite of fear is said to be courage. Fear is a mindset. Courage is an action. What do you fear? Do you find yourself overwhelmed by thoughts of things that might keep you from enjoying a higher level of success? Do you experience difficulty in focusing on things other than what you are afraid of? Are your fears the primary force behind your decisions and your behavior on the athletic field?

Do you know what we have discovered about fear? Most of us are incredibly unaware of our vulnerability to it. We rarely consciously think about our fears, do we?

There is little question that fear is a real factor in keeping athletes from maximizing potential. Too many young athletes become paralyzed by the fear of what might happen if they choose do this, or not do that. Whatever the root cause, when fear gets a foot in the door, it will keep you from searching for a route where you can create something better.

We hope this is what you hear us saying: It is one thing to fear, because fear can initially heighten our senses and makes us more aware of our surroundings. But it is quite another to let ourselves be led by our fears, to let "fear develop into the captain of our souls."

At the very core of the ability to confront fears is the strength of courage to look at the consequences of these fears and realize there is nothing faced that cannot be overcome. You don't need courage to handle what you already know how to do. You need courage to confront the uncertainty of what you have yet faced. Courage is the quality of being ready and willing to face the unknown situations that can—and will--arise in sports.

The sports experience carries the seeds of fear, but also in every fearful situation is the chance to create something better. The key is in having the courage to confront it…and perform despite it. Showing courage is often thought of as facing such situations without fear, but it also involves facing them despite fear.

"Courage doesn't mean that you have the strength to go on,
It simply means you go even when you don't have the strength."
-Thomas Kearse

Endurance

Endurance is one of the main ingredients in successful athletic performance. Endurance encompasses two major activity functions: muscular endurance and cardiovascular endurance. These two forms of endurance create a foundation for sustained activity during high intensity sports participation.

Muscular endurance describes your muscles' ability to continuously engage efficiently and effectively in extreme competitive situations, for as long as possible. Muscle endurance is a combination of strength and stamina. It describes how long you can maintain a high level of muscle performance without becoming fatigued.

The technique and method used today is quite different for developing both types of endurance. In developing muscular endurance, weight training is the most important component. But no matter how much drive and force you apply during workouts, it is useless if your energy is wasted on improper and inefficient exercises.

The technique we are talking about here is highly sports specific. Weight training instructors can assist in developing movement efficiency where effort is geared toward those muscles used in performing your role or position on the team.

Muscular endurance is similar to cardiovascular endurance, but there are differences. You see, cardiovascular endurance, also known as "cardio development" deals with your heart's and lungs' ability to deliver oxygen to your muscle tissue. We both remember the abundance of wind sprints we had to run after practice for "cardio development."

Cardio development leads to greater endurance when your heart is strong and actively pumping blood that results in more energy and less fatigue. Cardio endurance increases your blood flow to all the parts of your body, enhancing your ability to keep on going and augmenting your overall physicality.

What matters most with endurance is movement efficiency and sustained effort. Spending more time developing your muscles and building your cardio makes a huge difference late in a tough game or match. The level of your effort is more powerful and more efficient when both forms of endurance are at a high level.

Energy

The good old dictionary defines energy in this manner: "The strength and vitality required for sustained physical or mental activity." One of the first rules of sustained performance is the availability of energized power. Just like the energized bunny, you keep on ticking.

Energy is one of those things that you either have, or don't have. Your capacity for vigorous activity depends in large part on developing your energy level. Energy is a derivative of diet, rest, and workout routine. Without great energy the extent of your viability to perform with vigor and power from start to finish will be diminished.

What can you do in those times when you feel less energetic to develop more energy? Here are some suggestions:

- THINK ENERGY. The first lesson in releasing energy is to think ENERGY. Within is enough energy to do what you need to do--and what you want to do. All you have to do is to access it. That begins with thinking energy in your less than energetic moments, and the first thing you know energy will reappear.
- HAVE A SENSE OF PURPOSE. The more you are aligned with your purpose of playing your very best every game, you will experience an output of greater energy. Being specific in where you are headed and what you want to accomplish, will also create the availability of more energy to get it done.
- STAY ACTIVE. Energetic players don't waste their time in unproductive thought and activity. They don't sit around using up energy worrying about a coming event. They stay focused on positive outcomes. Their theme is the "more I do, the more I have to do with."

- STIMULATE ENERGY. You can stimulate energy through your body movements and posture. Run places even if you can walk. When you walk, do it at a brisk, purposeful pace. Look alive and alert. Appear dynamic in all of your activities. The key is to remind yourself that you are a bundle of energy.

Hustle

HUSTLE IS an indirect, yet decisive daily movement toward the pursuit of an upward path.

HUSTLE IS elbow grease, pushing and pulling, and solid effort.

HUSTLE IS doing all that is expected of you–even if there is not a coach around watching.

HUSTLE IS staying the course through grit and grime… sweat and tears… bumps and bruises.

HUSTLE IS having a strong work ethic to get a handle on any challenge, and then tackling it with the best of your ability.

HUSTLE IS doing your best with conditions as you find them -- even if you would like to have a different set of conditions.

HUSTLE IS continuing to do something that all around you are absolutely certain cannot be done.

HUSTLE IS doing the little things that others would not think are worth doing... and doing them well.

HUSTLE IS going hard enough on your first wind to see if you have a second.

HUSTLE IS working hard to maximizing your strengths and minimizing your weaknesses.

HUSTLE IS doing the things you have to do -- when you must do them -- in order to make positive things happen.

HUSTLE IS the condition created when you get desire and enthusiasm moving in the same direction.

HUSTLE IS racing to fulfill a dream with no speed limit on the pursuit of excellence and generation of success.

HUSTLE IS in the words of the great coach, Vince Lombardi, "...that moment when you have worked your heart out and lie exhausted on the field of battle -- victorious."

Major in Minors

There is very little difference between being good and being great in sports. Being great is not necessarily made up of doing the big things -- even though they are important. The real difference in attaining greatness is measured by how enthusiastically you stretch out to perform the little things that other less successful athletes would not think to be worth doing. Never underestimate the bigness of little.

Being an elite athlete is nothing more than a lot of little things done well. In a very real way, don't be too big to do the little things that will make you big, if you want to make a dramatic impact in the sports world. Make no mistake about it: you must learn how to do the little things before you can do the big things that will make you big.

What we mean is everyday attention to little things is no little thing. Big opportunities tend to come when you make the most of the little ones. Progress is built on doing the little things you may have spent little time doing before.

You will only be as big as the little things that generally are the important things. So, never feel too big to do the little things that have a way of leading you to enjoy the big and best things of life. Here are some additional suggestions:

- Everyday attention to little things is no little thing.
- Little things make big things bigger.
- You will only be as big as the little things help you focus on the important things.
- Champions do the little things without being told to do them... and they keep on doing them.

The route to accomplishing something great is to encounter and conquer all of the little things that lead to greatness.

> "The only true measure of your success is the ratio between what you might be on one hand, and what you become on the other hand."
>
> -General Dwight Eisenhower

Anticipation

The most significant way to become a better performer during a game is to be the creator of the action, not the effect of it. This begins with being more mindful of the three things that are needed at all times to maximize your play: perception of the action, processing the action, and performing based on the action. Being highly effective in these three areas is dependent on maximizing your ability to anticipate.

Success in most sports is often measured in fractions of seconds. The ability to react quickly and effectively accelerates the decision-making process that can give you an edge in competitive situations. Anticipation of what might happen improves what we call reaction time.

Reaction time is simply the brief interval of time between the initiation of game or match action and the determination of how to react to that action. The one constant here is that a delay in anticipation, regardless of the situation, can make the difference in reaction time. For example, a football linebacker is a fraction of a second late in reacting to a play and misses a tackle that results in a big yardage gain.

What is the key to maximizing reaction time? While some athletes may have more innate response skills than others, the development of anticipatory skills is definitely something that improves reaction time. Quality anticipation requires attentive presence to the now moment. A constant and deepen moment-by-moment mindfulness during the game action, will lead to more appropriate and quicker responses. The lack of complete focus and concentration does have an effect on anticipation and, subsequently, reaction time in an adverse way. But when you anticipate what may happen you maximize reaction time.

The ideal way to become more anticipatory is to possess a more present-tense mindset. You can train yourself to think only of the here-and-now. Consciously think about how to keep your attention on the task at hand. The more you focus on the present, the more alert you are to the things that could happen, resulting in quicker reactions.

Whatever you are doing, focus on what possibilities may arise. Raise your attention and energy to the highest level possible in every moment you are involved in the action. This will enhance your consciousness and elevate your level of play. You will actually notice things you have not been thoughtful of before. Never underestimate the importance of anticipation.

Do Something Special

Give the team a sample of the best you--and do something special.

Use your body, your mind and your God-given talents--and do something special.

Take instruction well and apply what you learn with all your might--and do something special.

Let the role you play on the team be greater and finer than the beat of a heart--and do something special.

Play your role to the best of your ability every time you participate--and you will do something special.

Earn your right to be a part of something special--by being something special…starting right now.

Lucky You...

The luckiest players are those who recognize that luck is by design. They attract it by the very nature of their performance level. The evolutionary nature of luck is the better you perform and the more you believe you belong in the winners' circle, the luckier you get.

Luck is not some mystical force beyond your control. Luck resides at the corner of belief and activity. We truly believe there is a solid connection between your believability, your activity level, and the luck you experience.

What should you take away from this? Your own lucky breaks happen when you have spring in your step and create momentum which manifests luck. Carry this with you, luck is indeed a product of your own construction. You create luck by putting yourself into a position to experience luck.

> "Sometimes your bad luck is a wonderful stroke of good luck because of what it saved you from."
>
> Josh Billings

A SONNY MOMENT

Every elite athlete has mastered the game-changers mentioned in this chapter, at least to a favorable degree. These great attributes lay right at the core of the mindset for an elite athlete. Before I add a point of emphasis to these game-changers, I want to spend some time talking about what in my estimation constitutes an elite athlete.

We talk quite a bit about being an elite athlete in the book. There is an elite athlete look. I know it when I see it, but nonetheless is not easy to describe, but I am going to give it a go and provide my thoughts on what I believe creates an elite athlete.

Elite athletes are those who are greater performers than most athletes on a team, but they are not better than anyone else. Think about that for a minute. The role the elite athlete plays on a team is a step above the role of others, but the elite athlete knows without the quality efforts of his teammates, the role he has played has been basically futile.

Elite athletes are also those who have propelled themselves to embrace the rare luxury of excellence. They are a model of consistency. As someone so appropriately said, "Top performers produce a symphony of coordinated motions which renders their performance as being virtually fluid and almost effortlessly."

Elite athletes possess an even temperament. They have not only learned how to play at a higher level, they have learned how to conduct themselves on a higher plane, as well. They have an emotional handle on the tension and mental anguish that arises during competition.

Elite athletes demonstrate a great in-game presence. This can truly make a big difference in the performance level of a team. The ultimate test of being an elite athlete is the ability to impress your mark upon game action in such a way as to alter the direction of the action. That's what elevates the elite athlete to extraordinary heights. But even if the elite athlete exhibits Herculean efforts, it still rests with his teammates to work in unison to turn those efforts into victories.

I can promise you that if you want to stretch out for a higher level of performance, it goes beyond talent and ability. The road to elite athletic status is littered with gifted athletes who came up short of where their abilities indicated they could go. They failed to master the kind of mindset these game-changers can produce to reach elite athletic status.

On the other side, are the elite athletes who overcame significant deficits and disadvantages in talent and abilities. Through an intense work ethic and determination, they emerged as quality athletes. Others sustained a discouraging injury and had to struggle through rehabilitation. Because of these experiences, they had to call on many difference-making attributes to mentally prepare themselves for putting in the time and effort to rise above the challenges they had faced.

Here's an important point that I don't want you to miss: Maybe you will not be good enough to reach the next level as an athlete. But what you learn as you strive to reach the next level is the kind of mindset needed to excel in other areas of life. The business world is full of former athletes who brought that mindset into their careers.

The reason so many former athletes make great strides in the outside world is because they know what it takes to be successful. They flat out have a great work ethic and know how to put in the effort. Because they have created great performance habits, the application of those habits to the work world is just a natural step.

There are many athletes who reached the pinnacle of athletic success who had to overcome significant adversity to get there. I have seen countless players who were reaching toward the top of their game only to have their world turned upside down. Some ran into a mental hurdle where doubts set it and self-confidence diminished.

That brings to mind something elite athletes do that average athletes fail to do. They put in extra time and practice to perfect their skills. This attitude may not always make them better, but I guarantee it does not make them worse. The challenge is to wake up every morning hungry to get better. This attitude soon becomes a habit. It becomes a part of you. It's no longer something you do…it's who you are.

Chapter Sixteen

EMOTIONAL CONTROL

Others cannot make you lose emotional control, only you can do that to yourself.

Do you have a tendency to lose your temper when things don't go your way? Do you fly-off-the-handle when someone does something, or says something, you don't like? Do you easily become angry with yourself when you are not performing as well as you know that you can?

As you probe your own experiences, what can you say about the role emotions are playing in your sports experience—and in your life? How are you doing in the area of emotional control and stability? Are your emotions working for or against you? Are your emotions your best servant or your worst enemy?

To experience the breadth and depth of emotions comes with the territory in sports. Almost all that happens before, and much of what happens during and after a game, is interpreted at the emotional level.

The word "emotion" comes from the Latin word, "exmovere," meaning "to excite, stir up or to move." Emotions are a basic and essential part of being human. There is little question that emotional control is an essential priority in playing sports and maximizing your budding career as a player.

We are convinced that a high ***emotional quotient*** (EQ) in athletics will advance an athlete up the success ladder almost as quickly as a high IQ. Both are needed to be an elite athlete, but the very nature of athletics calls for emotional control and stability both on and off the field.

Lax emotional control can carry you further and further away from the mainstream of an enjoyable and successful athletic career.

Even Keel

It takes a concise mental effort to develop an earnest and steadfast outlook where you remain undisturbed in times of emotional stress. By not caving in to highly emotional situations, you enjoy a better presence of mind and clarity of judgment as you tackle your responsibilities. It is in this frame of mind you perform your best.

Do you need some assistance in attaining an efficient state of emotional control? If so, a deeper understanding of situations that create emotional extremes is a first, and important, step in this fact-gathering process. Armed with this awareness, you can begin to consciously do something about bringing balance to those expanded emotional boundaries. You can focus fully on tackling those emotional situations where you have a tendency to lose control. Awareness is the beginning. Following that up with action, or possibly inaction, is the next step, whichever is the case.

It is possible to participate and perform with poise on a regular basis, where your emotions work for you, not against you. Make more productive emotions a part of your in-game activity going forward. As you become more habitual in your effort to abate extreme emotional reactions, your need for conscious awareness lessens. Eventually, it becomes second nature. But there is no shortcut. You must be vigilant at all times to keep emotions in line.

What we hope you hear us saying is top performers do not get too over-charged. They have a calmness and easiness about themselves that serves to maintain emotional equilibrium in pressure-cooker type situations that are a significant part of any sport. They exercise composure in those situations where constraint is vital to achievement.

There is no question in our minds that it is possible to participate and perform at a high level with emotions working for you and not against you. Once you have become fully and consciously aware of how you respond in situations where you have experienced a tendency to lose control, you can work toward more productive emotions being a part of your activity going forward. As you become more habitual in your effort to curtail emotional reactions, the need for conscious awareness lessens.

Emotional Inhibitors

Speaking of negative emotions, there are over six hundred words that express negative feelings. Consequently, negative emotions are part of life. For some they tend to dominate their thought patterns. We hope that's not you. The depth of the reaction you internalize about negative situations could lead to unhealthy consequences.

Unpleasant feelings are just as crucial as the enjoyable ones in helping a player get a handle on the ups and downs of sports. If it wasn't for a few negative emotions now and then, you wouldn't enjoy the good ones as much, would you?

A word of caution: Attempting to suppress negative emotions can backfire and even diminish a sense of well-being. Instead of your backing away from negative emotions, it is crucial that you accept them and manage them. The way you deal with emotions, especially negative ones, have very important consequences. Emotions come. Emotions go. It is the aftermath that holds the key. Some negative emotions can take you down to depths that create negative issues.

As a general principle, it is essential to avoid emotional extremes, notably during game action. Highly emotional actions when carried to extremes can become a source of harm for a team. How many times have you seen a player celebrate after executing a great play, only to lose his focus and get burned on the next play?

This may make us look like we are too "old school" to appreciate the emotional excitement that players today exhibit after making a great play. Celebration is okay long as you don't lose sight of the fact it just was one play. It is our experience elite athletes expect to make great plays, so rarely do they undergo excessive celebratory reactions when they do. They turn their attention to the next action. Elite athletes seldom exhibit emotional reactions which end up hurting their team. They are vigilant at all times to keep negative emotions in line.

Positive emotions are healthy in attaining and maintaining mental stability. Conversely, research shows how you effectively go about handling negative emotions will also play a vital role in your personal well-being, as well as the well-being of the team.

If your inability to handle "negatives" is a concern for you, set a goal of working harder to gain a greater grip on how to handle harmful emotions. In those situations where you have experienced difficulty in maintaining effective emotional control, be solution-minded. What follows are ways to assist you in creating more emotional balance,

Relaxation

Much of sports success is about letting the game come to you.

A key factor in handling those "emotional-type situations" is found in the ability to relax. Relaxation is a process that decreases the effects of emotional stress and anxiety on your mind and body. Many outstanding athletes have had their careers cut short because of an inability to handle elevated emotional conditions. Over time the tension generated by stress and tension had a negative effect on their bodies. It led to injury and various health issues.

We are firm believers that learning how to properly employ relaxation techniques can help you cope with pre-game stress and with stress-related game situations. Relaxation may be as important to improving athletic performance as any undertaking. No question, you can benefit from learning relaxation techniques if you have a tendency to get uptight before a game or during the course of a game.

Relaxation is a skill. It is something you can train your mind and body to do. Learning basic relaxation techniques is simple and easy. As with any form of skill development, relaxation techniques are improved with practice.

Two thoughts before moving on to the techniques: First, be patient with yourself. Don't let your effort to practice relaxation techniques become yet another stress source. Second, if one relaxation technique doesn't work for you, try another technique. We discuss three here:

Visualization. In this relaxation technique, you take a visual journey where your focus is on your role and the activity you will be engaged in, not on the results of that activity. The results you want will be there when you clear your mind of excess tension, relax and visualize successfully performing your role and making all the right moves.

This is a good technique to use pre-game. You may want to close your eyes, sit in a quiet spot, loosen any tight clothing, and listen to some soothing music. The aim is to focus on the present and visualize positive actions.

Muscle Relaxation. In this relaxation technique, you focus on slowly tensing and then relaxing each muscle group. This can help your awareness as to the difference between muscle tension and normal relaxation. Muscle relaxation starts by tensing and relaxing the muscles in groups from your toes way up to your head. You can also start with your head and neck and work down to your toes. Focus on tensing your muscles for about five seconds and then relax for 30 seconds, and repeat.

Deep Breathing. When you feel a "rush" racing through your body, there is an ageless, but simple breathing exercise which can dissipate stress both mentally and physically. While the deep breathing technique is incredibly beneficial for the body, many see it as a great way to relax the mind and the body

There are three dimensions you can use in improving the ability to relax through proper deep breathing: The first lesson is to shut your mouth. Secondly, slowly draw in a good deep breath through your nose. Then thirdly, exhale slowly through your mouth. The pace at which you breathe, and the manner of how you breathe, will enhance your ability to relax in tense situations.

Relax and remember this too shall pass…
Peace of mind holds you in good stead all the time.

Dr. Wayne Dyer

Provide others peace of mind,
not a piece of your mind.

"It's Okay" Attitude

The first law in tackling any challenge is to view it as being okay.

One of the best ways to maximize emotional control is to key in on an "It's okay" attitude. This attitude is built on the premise if there is nothing you can do about a situation, then why should you get emotionally involved with it?

Few of us are immune to the little things that can get under our skin and endanger our emotional well-being. How do you react when a teammate doesn't do what they said they were going to do...you are late for practice and the driver in front of you is going ten miles below the speed limit...that misassignment the coach got in your face about? Did you get internally upset and react in emotional way? Does your blowing your stack change any of these conditions? We doubt it.

Isn't it really okay for the world to move and act at its own pace? If you get upset, what have you achieved? What have you truly accomplished with this kind of action? The only thing you accomplish is the fact you have let someone or something consciously or unconsciously knock you right out of an "It's okay" state of mind.

You can get upset, angry, feel miserable, but guess what? It doesn't change the reality of the situation, does it? For example, those who worry about weight focus on the weight, not on the solution. By picturing the weight issue continuously in their minds, what obese people get is more weight. Do you understand the principal here? Worry will give you something to do, but it won't get you anywhere.

When we allow our problems to be okay, we have positioned ourselves to move beyond the problem and begin the process of seeking an answer or solution. The goal is simple: adjust to the realities of life, regardless of how unfair these realities appear to be. An "It's okay" attitude helps us realize if there is nothing we can do about circumstances, we are not going to let it concern us. A wise decision is to remember that if something is none of our business, we should work hard to keep it that way.

A roommate of mine (Lou) in pro baseball often used the term, "You gotta cooperate with the inevitable." Learn to go with the flow. Let things be. "Cooperate with the inevitable." Establish an "It's okay" attitude. If you do, you will last longer and go further.

Keep Your Cool

We don't mean to make light of "keeping your cool," but here are some humorous ideas from various unknown sources that can help:

- The more you grow up, the less you will blow up.
- Flying into a rage always results in unsafe landings.
- Those who are always exploding rarely end up being big shots.
- It's more tasteful to swallow angry words before we say them than to eat them afterward.
- Those who lose their heads are the last to realize it.
- We are more apt to remain calm and collected when we show restraint in shooting from the lip.
- We contribute to the world's pollution problem when we blow our stacks.
- The trouble with letting off steam is that it only gets us into more hot water.
- Others find out what kind of minds we have when we give them a piece of it.
- Before giving someone a piece of your mind, just make sure you can get by with what's left.
- Striking while the iron is hot is good… striking while the head is hot -- is <u>not</u>.

To reach a new level of performance take control of your emotions.

"Butterflies"

The emotional experience that really stands out is the pre-game "butterflies" which buzz around in your stomach prior to a game. The "butterflies" arise from the feeling you are excited and ready to get the game started.

Whatever you do, refrain from thinking of those flutters in your stomach as a basic and functional negative factor. There's a tendency to misinterpret this case of "nerves" in a pessimistic way. You might begin to question whether you are capable of matching up with your opponent, or if you are adequately prepared to compete.

Think of the "butterflies" you experience as a plus. They are a great servant. They work on your behalf. They are a positive sign that you are mentally and physically ready to perform. So, don't fight the "butterflies." Let them work for you… not against you.

Think realistically. Learn to put things in perspective--not getting too high or too low--when confronted with a challenge. Balance is the answer.

Taking Things in Stride

As we close this chapter, it is worthy to look at some things that will help to fight emotional disparities:

- Manage time wisely. Controlling your time rather than having your time control you, aids greatly in controlling emotions. The time control factor lines up this way: Plan. Prepare. Practice. Perform. This is the order of events to effectively limit emotional reactions.
- See problems as opportunities. Focus on solutions. When you look beyond your problems, you see a world of opportunity.
- Prepare for key events. Preparing mentally, emotionally, and physically for important events helps you to stay calm in those situations where tension tends to ride high.

A SONNY MOMENT

"Trash talking" is one of the those things that comes with the territory in athletics--particularly at the higher levels of play. There's plenty of "smack" that goes on between opposing players. An athlete has to have a thick skin if he is to survive the adverse and hostile rhetoric that can come his way.

When someone says something to you or about you, how do you react to it? If you let the words of others get under your skin, you lose your focus. The focus shifts to you and your feelings, away from the task or situation at hand. Grasp that principal. It's important.

If words can control you, then just about everything else can. "Trash talk" exists because it allows players on opposing teams the use of a "bully pulpit*"* where they employ negative language toward each other, hopefully to get an emotional reaction that will give one or the other an edge going forward.

In the sports world, negative rhetoric can sometimes be thick and vicious. The comments you receive are even more intense the better you become as an athlete. It has been my experience when you reach elite status as an athlete, you have learned how to take a deep breath, laugh it off and go on about your business in a quality manner. Otherwise, you will as the old saying goes, "let someone get to you."

Not all "trash talk" comes from opponents, either. Sometimes a teammate or teammates can put a dig or two into another teammate. Notably this happens when that teammate is performing really well. I believe jealousy plays a role in this situation, but the elite athlete shrugs it off and continues to focus and perform well.

There is a very delicate balance here. There is no way to separate who you are from what someone says you are, if you take the negative bait. I can assure you cannot perform like the athlete you want to be if you let "trash talk" get into your head.

Here's a couple of things I want you to keep in mind: Don't ask yourself, "Why is this person 'bad-mouthing' me? Asking 'why' isn't an appropriate question to ask yourself. Just thinking about it gives your opponent an advantage. You lose focus...it can take you away from your purpose of playing your best on every play.

If you get into a "trash talking" contest with an opponent who is really good at it, he will drag you down to his level and beat you with his experience. The smart move is to smile and go on and do your job to the best of your ability.

What I hope you hear me saying is words can only hurt you if you let them. Words that come off someone else's lips speak volumes about you if it affects your play. If you let it, it could become a part of your reality. Regardless, if the "trash talk" comes from an opponent or a teammate, always keep in mind that what is said to you about you, should mean absolutely nothing to you. It cannot change the level of your play, unless you permit it.

Finally, let me say that I was not a big proponent of "trash talking" by my own players. I think there is a tendency to lose sight of your purpose of playing your best on every play. There seems to be an emotional shift away from that purpose toward a more personal thing with the opposing player. When you get yourself so emotionally entwined with that player, the next thing you know he has beaten you. What good has all that "trash talking" done for you then?

***

While we are on the topic of emotional responses, there is something that can engender some highly emotional reactions in coaches. It comes through the form of critics. The life of a coach is to encounter those who can be highly critical with criticism—the kind of criticism which can be severely emotional and very harsh. Winning grants no protection whatsoever from severe critique. Win or lose, criticism can come from fans, media and even disgruntled players.

I feel reasonable certain that coaches perform their most courageous work when confronting the views of those who vehemently disagree with them. I appreciated the honest critics, mostly in the media, who might question something that had happened during a game or a coaching decision. I had respect for their position, toking a cooperative stance I would thank them for their interest in improving our program. But in the end, it was up to me to determine if the criticism had merit. Will it make us better? That was the question.

Normally, the toughest critics are the ones who come from the fan base. As a general rule, they have limited knowledge of what they are talking about. And thank goodness, most of those who holler the loudest are in the minority, and have a limited platform to voice their criticism.

Most of the fans who are highly critical, have little familiarity with what is necessary for the successful functioning of a quality program. They can latch onto a negative belief system--heart, soul, and body, thinking they know too much to listen to a realistic viewpoint.

You can hear what others have to say, but it is wise to listen only to those who know what they are talking about…who have been there and done it. There are things that can only be learned if one has been in the hot seat. You just can't get it or have it any other way in my book.

Here's my recommendation for dealing with the vocal critics: Pay them little mind, but don't ignore them. I have learned that if you thank them for their critique, you take the curse off the situation. *"I really appreciate your input, but..."* The old "yes, but," answer puts you back in the driver's seat...at least temporarily anyway.

Critics are not always found outside the locker room. There are players who blame the coaching staff for their poor performance or lack of playing time. They bend everyone else's ear around them about how bad they have been treated. Get on top of this situation early on. Rarely does it go away on its own.

PART

V

OVERTIME

SONNY'S BEST… ALL ABOUT WINNING

Winning is the bottom line. It is why you go through all the preparatory things presented in the previous chapters. In life there are always winners and losers I believe winning plays a vital role in your becoming a fully integrated person—a person ready to tackle whatever life presents to you…and do it on your terms.

In this chapter I offer a lot of reminders about why winning is so important. These are the kinds of things you or your coach can copy and put in a place where they can be a constant reminder. Don't let anyone tell you that your human drive to win will be anything but crucial. Sports and life are all about creating a winning culture.

"Winning may not be everything… but it does beat anything that finishes in second place."
Paul (Bear) Bryant

WINNING COMES FROM…

WINNING comes from a Challenge……….accept it.

WINNING comes from an Adventure…..........dare it.

WINNING comes from an Opportunity…........take it.

WINNING comes from a Mystery…….........unfold it.

WINNING comes from being Demanding........face it.

WINNING comes from tackling a Puzzle.......solve it.

WINNING comes from taking a Risk…..undertake it.

WINNING comes from reaching a Goal.....achieve it.

WINNING comes from an Experience…..…enjoy it.

WINNING comes from a Mission…....……..fulfill it.

WINNING comes from a Mindset……..…develop it.

ANATOMY OF WINNERS'

Winners' realize winning is not everything, but striving to win is.

Winners' have a badge of honor of doing their best... giving the most they have...being productive to the peak of your capacity.

Winners' mentally paint big pictures and then work to turn those pictures into reality.

Winners' set stretch goals and work relentlessly toward making them a reality.

Winners' adopt a code of conduct of high standards of thought and behavior and hold these standards sacred--without succumbing to pressure to change them.

Winners' desire things from themselves as well as desire things for themselves. They believe that to receive something they must give something... and the giving always comes first.

Winners' recognize that winning is something they experience on the inside, not something they have on the outside. It is measured by what they hold in their hearts, not in their hands.

Winners' are always thankful for what they have, then do their best to make it better.

Winners' possess the belief that to count for something special to others, you must first count for something special to yourself.

Winners' move forward as if the limits of what they are capable of doing does not exist.

Winners' carry the feeling that they are doing what their hearts desires... and doing it well.

Winners' appreciate that winning is important--otherwise, why are their blue ribbons?

-Adapted from several sources

WINNING IS ABOUT RESULTS

Winning is not about how you look--even though how you look helps you to feel like a winner.

Winning is not about the knowledge level that you have--although you couldn't perform well without it.

Winning is not about the skills you acquire -- even though your skills set contributes greatly to winning.

Winning is not about how you perform -- even though your performance is vitally important to winning.

Winning is about results…the kind of results you want happen over time, not overnight; but the questions are these: Did you get the results you wanted? Did you make it to podium to receive the trophy?

WANT TO WIN?

If a team wants to WIN...

Believes it can WIN...

Prepares itself to WIN...

Sees itself WINNING...

Commits itself to WINNING...

Performs like a WINNER...

Then what beyond itself is there

To keep it from winning?

-Adapted from an unknown source

"Winners never take time to learn the meaning of defeat."
-General James Mathis

WHAT WINNERS' DO

- Winners proceed as if the limits to their capabilities do not exist…they are always attempting to make something happen… sitting back and waiting is not their trademark.
- Winners are creators of circumstances, not victims of circumstances…they are not trapped by routine or do they cling to the familiar when something better is within reach.
- Winners recognize that if they are not making a few mistakes along the way, they are not making much of anything else either.
- Winners realize that it is not possible to win at a high level without staring losing in the eye and risk trying to win.
- Winners work on the theory that if you are willing to accept the risk of losing, the odds of winning will work in your favor.
- Winners see that the more exposure they have to winning opportunities, the more chances they have to be successful.
- Winners don't worry about failing... they think about the chances they miss if they fail to make the attempt.
- Winners believe it will be difficult to be good at anything they do unless they attempt to be good at everything they do.
- Winners don't wait for chances they take them. They appreciate if they are going to miss, make it a big miss.
- Winners live with the supportive feeling that they will always strive to make something happen. Around a winners' locker room that attitude counts for something very special.

-Unknown source

Champions do their best in less critical situations, so they will respond with a higher impulse in more critical situations.

ROUTE TO VICTORY

If you appreciate that there is something better than you have ever experienced in sports...

If you have strong feelings about what you are doing… and work through your doubts and fears…

If you concern yourself with your own performance and focus on what you must do…

If you always try to do your best every time you are at practice or in a game…

If you discipline yourself to stay the course even when the odds are stacked against your team…

If you want to succeed badly enough and patiently work toward making daily improvement…

If you keep your focus on the present, and not let yesterday or tomorrow weigh you down…

If you are courageous enough to risk making things happen when things need to happen…

If you take the initiative to grow beyond your difficulties, and meet your challenges head on…

If you follow your dreams, and work hard and smart to maximize your physical resources…

If you tie a knot and hold on when you feel you are at the end of your rope…

If in the far reaches of your heart, you truly believe you have what it takes to be a winner…

The odds are in your favor to emerge as the victor in the greatest contest of all – the contest with yourself.

-Adapted from several sources

High achievers never confuse movement with progress. They stay focused on finding the right resources they need to activate successful result that moves the needle.

STEPS TO BEING A WINNER

Dream more than most think is practical…
Expect more than most think is wise…
Prepare better than most think is possible…
Risk more than most think is feasible…
Do more than most think is worthy…
and keep on doing it.
-Source unknown

"A team removes a big roadblock to winning when it learns there is a big difference between doing something and getting something done."

-Steve Spurrier

One of the givens of athletics is that you are constantly meeting a new opponent who brings a new challenge. The significance of moving on to the next opportunity with continual momentum requires a richer recognition of looking forward with anticipation, not backward with celebratory reflection.

"The most important thing that comes from winning are not things."
-Lavell Edwards

"If you believe in yourself and have dedication and pride – and never quit, you'll be a winner. The price of victory is high – but so are the rewards."
-Paul (Bear) Bryant

"I can be a winner" is the vision.

"I will work to be a winner" is the price.

"I will be a winner" is the ticket.

"I am a winner" is the prize.

-Adapted from an unknown source

BEING NUMBER ONE...

First and foremost, possess a commitment to be the best athlete you possibly can be.

Have a clear direction—not scattered vision--of where you are going and why you want to go that way.

Possess discipline and self-mastery to distant yourself from intolerance and over-indulgence in things that harm the body, mind and soul.

Prepare yourself with an education and acquiring expertise that will set you above.

Realize that there is only one option when it comes to the process to success--being committed it…in-between is not an option.

Appreciate that results obtained are a direct reflection of your best effort to honor the process to success established by the coaches.

Demonstrate leadership which prompts others to readily accept and follow your direction and actions.

Being number one is making the decision that you will always attempt to come through…every moment you are participating.

-Selected from numerous sources

"Winning is a validation; it means all of the sweat, hustle, practice time, playing hard and smart has paid off."

-Jimmy Johnson

WINNING FORMULA

Keep your THOUGHTS positive,
Because your THOUGHTS become
your ACTIONS.
Keep your ACTIONS positive…
Because your ACTIONS become
your HABITS.
Keep your HABITS positive,
Because your HABITS become
your PERFORMANCE BASE.
Keep your PERFORMANCE BASE positive,
Because your PERFORMANCE BASE
becomes your WINNING FORMULA.
-Adapted from an unknown author

A FINAL WORD

Winning the "head" game is a personal choice. It makes little difference where you are in your development right now. What is important is the great discovery you have made about yourself as we have journeyed through the book together and the gigantic steps you have already taken toward realizing your real potential. In a very real way, we believe this is the beginning of a new ending for you. We celebrate that you are ready to go.

The one thing we have discovered over these years is the opportunities for growth that are presented to you as an athlete become more prevalent the more actively you create and pursue opportunities. Some of these opportunities come from experience. Some comes from experimenting. Some come from example. Some come from making errors. Some come from unexpected places. But they all come when you are energetic and enthusiastically hustling to find them.

So, now as you prepare to leave us and ride off from what you are today to seek what you will become tomorrow, the mystery and adventure of the journey is in great hands—your own. Keep training, keep practicing. Keep hustling. Keep improving. But also keep this book close at hand. Whether in sports—or in life—this book can serve as an authentic reference source for your future. The nature of this book requires the gift of presence. It demands the gift of action. Up to it?

Whatever

Whatever helps you to achieve your vision and dreams…
Whatever ignites your best passion and commitment…
Whatever stirs your inner motivation and deepest being…
Whatever builds confidence in handling your toughest tests…
Whatever warms your heart and expands your mind…
Whatever you desire, that's what we desire for you.

Sonny
Lou

ACKNOWLEDGMENTS

An undertaking of this type and size requires the involvement of countless people. We would like send a shout out to those who took the time and effort to help us make this a reality.

Not only did many of those who were asked to provide a review do just that, but they took the time to do some editing and offer some judicious recommendations.

Then there is Aubrey Whitaker, a retired teacher and coach. Aubrey jumped all over this project with his editing pin. It's amazing how some people are able to find the miss use of a word here and usage of an improper tense there. Aubrey's forty plus years in a classroom and on an athletic field was a valuable, if not surprising, assist for us.

We send out a big thanks to Denny Kearley, Priscilla Wilder, and Wendall Walker, all who made salient input.

We especially thank Dana Vickery for the design of a beautiful cover and her usual insightful commentary about the book content.

We thank anyone we have overlooked. It was not intentional. Your encouragement, criticism, patience, and most of all, your tremendous support was often timely and much needed.

About Lou Vickery...

Lou Vickery has had four distinct careers:

- A professional baseball player
- Stockbroker for Merrill Lynch
- Professional sales and marketing trainer
- Radio and TV show host

Being a long-time author would make it five.

` After graduating from Escambia County High School in Atmore, Alabama, Lou signed a professional baseball contract with the St. Louis Cardinals. Over a nine-year career, Lou played in both the Cardinal and the New York Yankees organizations.

Lou got his B.S. degree from Troy State University (AL), graduating after his baseball career. He coached a year in Troy, then spent four years with Merrill Lynch as an Account Executive. Lou moved into the training and development field with Pat Ryan and Associates of Chicago, Ill. in l974. After 1980, he did contract training for numerous national organizations, including Universal Underwriters, and over a thirty (30) year period worked with over 2,800 companies in 44 states and two foreign countries. Lou has spoken in every city in the USA with a population of over 150,000.

After his retirement from the training business, Lou spent 14 years as a co-host and host of a talk radio show. More recently, he has been the host of UPTALKTV.

Lou is the author of fifteen books. Those books presently in print can be found at amazon.com or louvickerybooks.com.

Made in the USA
Las Vegas, NV
22 November 2021

35022396R00132